More Advance Praise for
Kidgets: and other insightful stories about quality in education

"Getting people to change their paradigms is not an easy task. They have questions such as, 'What's wrong with the way we do it now?' and 'How will it work out?' They need help in visualizing what might happen if they were to let go of their current view of the world, how 'things ought to be' and they need to strengthen their will to make changes. These stories by Maury Cotter and Daniel Seymour do just that. They entertain and they instruct. They give examples and they raise troubling questions. Be careful. They might just get past your defenses."

Myron Tribus
Quality Counselor

"This book is an important companion to helping us change the way we think about how children learn."

Dawna Markova
Author of *How Your Child* Is *Smart*

"Finally, a book that illustrates real-life applications for the theories I've been learning in the class-rooms. I would definitely recommend it to any individual entering the education field."

Amy Atkinson
Student, secondary education major
University of Wisconsin-Madison

"The primary customer of the school is the student. Kidgets *reminds us of that fact."*

Franklin Schargel
Quality Coordinator
George Westinghouse Vocational Technical High School
Brooklyn, New York

"Dr. Deming taught me that my purpose in teaching should be to instill in my students a 'yearning for learning.' Whether quality in education is living to learn or learning to live in a quality way, Kidgets, *through its vignettes, captures the essence of what I believe 'yearning for learning' is all about."*

Theresa May Hicks
Elementary Teacher
Wilmington, Ohio
$10,000 Deming Research Grant Recipient

Kidgets

Also available from ASQC Quality Press

Total Quality for Schools: A Suggestion for American Education
Joseph C. Fields

Quality Education
Gray Rinehart

A *Quality System for Education*
Stanley J. Spanbauer

To receive a complimentary catalog of publications, call 800-248-1946.

Kidgets

and other insightful stories
about quality in education

Maury Cotter
and
Daniel Seymour

ASQC Quality Press
Milwaukee, Wisconsin

Kidgets: And Other Insightful Stories About Quality in Education
Maury Cotter and Daniel Seymour

Library of Congress Cataloging-in-Publication Data
Cotter, Maury.
    Kidgets : and other insightful stories about quality in education
/ Maury Cotter and Daniel Seymour.
        p.   cm.
    Includes bibliographical references.
    ISBN 0-87389-248-8 (alk. paper)
    1. School management and organization—United States—Case
studies.   2. Education—United States—Case studies.   I. Seymour,
Daniel.   II. Title.
LB2806.C679   1993
371.2'00973—dc20   93-27803
                                                        CIP

"Hunting for Worms" is reprinted with permission from Daniel Seymour and Terry Seymour, *America's Best Classrooms* (Peterson's: Princeton, N.J., 1992).

10 9 8 7 6 5 4 3 2 1

ISBN 0-87389-248-8

Acquisitions Editor: Susan Westergard
Project Editor: Kelley Cardinal
Production Editor: Annette Wall
Marketing Administrator: Mark Olson
Set in Caslon 540 by Montgomery Media, Inc.
Illustrations and cover by Dale Mann.
Printed and bound by BookCrafters, Inc.

ASQC Mission: To facilitate continuous improvement and increase customer satisfaction by identifying, communicating, and promoting the use of quality principles, concepts, and technologies; and thereby be recognized throughout the world as the leading authority on, and champion for, quality.

For a free copy of the ASQC Quality Press Publications Catalog, including ASQC membership information, call 800-248-1946.

Printed in the United States of America.

 Printed on acid-free recycled paper

 ASQC
Quality Press
611 East Wisconsin Avenue
Milwaukee, Wisconsin 53202

The only thing that keeps us from floating off with the wind is our stories.

—Tom Spanbauer
The Man Who Fell in Love with the Moon

Storyboard

Getting Started

The Stories

More Ideas

Acknowledgments

We have many to thank: Andy Hollinger for touching young people's lives with his passion for art; Terry Seymour—author, teacher, brother, and TOPP Team member; David Briggs for sharing with us the stories of JJ and the student-centered cafeteria workers at Alhambra High School; Edmonds School District's lead goose, Brian Benzel; David Porter—colonel, helicopter pilot, behavioral scientist, and Winnie-the-Pooh aficionado; that worm-hunting, award-winning Minnesota Teacher of the Year James Ellingson; and William Feddersen for knowing what's good, better, best.

We also thank Elaine Biech, the mother of a dinosaur-loving boy; Carrie Valentine, who looks into the heart and mind of each child and noticed a notebook in the way and a policy that dropped kids; students Nicolo LaMasa, Keyur Parikh, and Brenda DeJesus, who approach learning from complementary angles; John Pierzchalski for wrestling out his budget; Franklin Schargel for giving Maggie what she needed; Linda Barrows and her team, who are eliminating "butts" and saying "not yet" as they help each child reach for mastery;

David Langford, an education pioneer with a daughter who needed to borrow a reading book for the summer; Anne and Bill Conzemius, who told dozens of stories that inspired Kidgets; and Adam Cotter, who is definitely "okay."

These people are the everyday heroes. And we hope their stories will give life to new and important directions for education in America.

In addition to those who told stories, several others guided our thinking and writing, including W. Edwards Deming, Myron Tribus, Enid Hilton Brown, Theresa May Hicks, Jan O'Neill, Warren Gaskill, and Kelly Cotter. A special thanks to John Cotter and Ray Seymour for continuous help and support.

Introduction

When David Langford, education pioneer and consultant, begins a speech on education, he often asks how many people in the room have ever gone to school. When everyone raises their hands, he says, "Oh good, then I must have the right room."

We are all in that "right room," because education is central to all our lives. When we ask what is needed to appreciate diversity in our society, we answer "education." When we ask what is needed to promote peace, we answer "education." Education is not just about a first grader learning to read or a high school junior memorizing the table of elements. It is about improving life and living.

Education in America needs help. It was designed to produce workers for farms, then workers for factories. The world has changed. Schools have changed, too, but not nearly as much. A serious gap has developed.

Who's to blame? No one, and everyone, but that's not the issue. Everyone will be needed to make it better.

This is a book about improving quality in education. Does that mean we don't have quality now?

No. It means no matter how good we are, we can always improve. And if we don't learn how to improve rapidly in a rapidly changing world, our schools and our children will be at risk. Small, gradual improvements are not enough for the issues and challenges now facing education. We need an approach that enables rapid change, a major shift in how quickly we progress.

So, how do we learn to improve rapidly? The approach we present in this book is called total quality management (TQM) by some, continuous quality improvement (CQI) by others. Its origins go back to the 1930s and the use of statistical-control methods to improve industrial processes. It migrated after World War II to Japan under the watchful eyes of two Americans: Dr. W. Edwards Deming and Dr. Joseph Juran. There the focus broadened considerably. It took a humanistic turn. Quality became an organizational driving force that could only be achieved by an educated, motivated, and empowered work force.

The notion of quality changed in other ways as well. It went from something that was viewed as static to something that was ever-changing. The new view suggested that you can always improve, always find a better way. The old way tended to portray quality in very individualistic terms. But if you began to look at work as a process, you quickly understood that to improve a process you needed input from everyone involved in that process. The mechanisms to pursue quality changed as well.

The scientific method was introduced: hypotheses were generated, data collected, and rigorous problem-solving techniques used.

And perhaps most important, the very definition of quality changed. The traditional definition was based upon an intrinsic belief that artisans or craftspersons define and deliver quality according to their own standards. They know it when they see it. In contrast, the TQM philosophy suggests that the person who uses or benefits from the work is the one who defines quality. It is their expectations or requirements that need to be met, not just your own.

More than a decade ago now, TQM reemerged on the American industrial scene. Xerox, Ford, and Procter and Gamble, among many others, began applying the philosophy and tools to their operations. Then followed the service sector: Federal Express; the city of Madison, Wisconsin; Hospital Corporation of America; the University of Maryland; and El Camino College. Each organization took what it needed and adapted it to its own special circumstances.

Now we are seeing the philosophy going through another metamorphosis—this time in K–12 education. Pioneering efforts are taking place in schools around the nation: Sitka, Alaska; Wilmington, Ohio; Pasadena, Texas; and Brooklyn, New York. And these schools are experiencing results that leapfrog improvements made through other means.

In this book our aim is to create a basic understanding of some of the modern concepts of quality. To do this we use stories. This is not a "how to" book. It is a book aimed at illustrating concepts by connecting them to your world. We have used stories to do that because we believe in their power. Any general concept, principle, rule, or theory comes from a collection of incidents or stories. So, if you really want to understand a concept at its roots, begin at the beginning with the stories. Each story may contain one message, or many. As with any story, what is learned will depend largely on what the reader is ready to learn. And so, this book will be different for each reader.

We have divided this book into three parts: "Getting Started," "The Stories," and "More Ideas." In the first part, we present a section called "Quality: The Key Concepts." This section sets the stage for the stories by giving the reader a basic description of ten quality concepts that we think have specific relevance to teaching and learning in K–12. You will need a general understanding of these concepts before you move on in the book. You do not need to become a TQM expert, however, so don't expect more than a brief overview.

A matrix follows this section and shows which of the book's stories correspond with which concepts. You will notice that each story illustrates more than one concept and that each concept is illustrated by more than one story. This chart can aid you in getting the most out of the stories as you use them in discussion and education settings.

Following the matrix is "A Story About Stories—Brother Rick." It illustrates the power of story telling.

The core of the book lies in the stories themselves. These tales come from real people, from California to New York to Alaska to Texas. They come from kindergartners through high school seniors, from teachers, counselors, principals, superintendents, parents, custodians, cooks, and secretaries. We asked all these people to tell us their stories. From a rich store, we chose a selection to illustrate the key quality concepts.

At the end of each story are discussion-starter questions. These questions can be used to help connect the stories to quality concepts and to your school. They are very effective in a classroom, meeting, or workshop environment. You might try having people read a given story. Then toss out the discussion starters and see where it takes you. We hear over and over how this helps people begin to discuss openly some of the real barriers and possibilities in their own schools and school systems.

The final section is called "More Ideas." As we mentioned, this is not a "how to" book. It is very short on technical details and implementation plans.

Our goal is to entice and excite. If we accomplish our goal, then we're certain you'll want to know more. And that is the purpose of this final section. There you will find references to books, videos, networks, and other resources to help you continue your journey.

Getting Started

Quality: The Key Concepts

The stories included in this book present ways to think about quality concepts in a school setting. To aid in your thinking and discussions, we first offer a short description of the concepts and then provide a list of stories that illustrate those concepts. Also, see the matrix at the end of this section for a handy cross reference.

Developing a Customer Orientation

What is quality? To define quality you have to ask those people your products or services are intended to benefit. The owner of a toaster decides if it is a quality toaster. The patient decides whether she is getting quality hospital care. So, first you identify those people who use or benefit from your output— that is, your customers. Then you ask your customers about their requirements, their expectations. Finally, you apply your expertise to interpret or convert the desires being expressed into a product or service that not only meets but exceeds your customers' expectations. That's developing a customer orientation.

Who is education intended to benefit? Students, primarily, of course. But in a much different sense than the toaster buyer. We can't just ask a first grader what he or she needs to learn. But we can ask for and observe their wants and needs, and we can apply our expertise to meeting or exceeding their needs. Their wants may include features we can't afford. But meeting their needs must be our relentless aim. In addition to students, there are other "customers": parents, businesses who hire our graduates, and colleges who admit them as first-year students. As we look further at processes within education, we find that the fifth-grade teacher is a customer of the fourth-grade teacher, and everyone in the school is a customer of the lunchroom. Ultimately, society is a customer of the whole process. Do we view these people as customers now? What do these customers want, expect, and most of all, need? And then, how can we transform our processes and systems to exceed those needs?

Stories About Customer Orientation

Meeting Maggie's Needs
Kitchen Duty
Making Small Problems Big
Will the Real Customer Please Stand Up?
JJ

Aiming at a Clear Mission and Vision

Each day we work hard. The clock starts. Paper, parts, ideas move from the in basket to the out basket. The clock stops. What did we accomplish? For whom? What is the purpose of our work? A clear sense of mission and vision helps us feel a sense of accomplishment. It also helps us aim our work more effectively. Without a sense of direction and design, policies are set and procedures are generated that may block the real purpose of our work.

What are the mission and vision of our schools? Do we simply want to see kids graduate? What will a mission like that accomplish? Will it just lead us to make sure they pass and get a diploma? Or, is our mission to control kids and ensure they follow all the rules? Is it to have students demonstrate they know a given body of facts? Is it to instill an appreciation for lifelong learning? Any policy you make—whether for borrowing books or feeding kids—should be designed according to where you are aiming.

Stories About Mission and Vision

Kidgets

Not Yet

Kitchen Duty

Will the Real Customer Please Stand Up?

Continuously Improving Everything We Do

All of us have a tendency to fall into routines or ruts that box in our views of how to do things. We do them the way we have always done them, not bothering to stretch our minds to think of ways to improve. We're too busy, and besides, "Why fix it if it ain't broke?" Yet one of the keys to life and to a healthy organization is to pursue, relentlessly, a better way. There is always a more elegant solution, a more effective process.

A high school English teacher loves to teach Shakespeare. She has been doing it for ten years. Do her students love it, too? Does she know? Does she have a system for finding out and then testing out new teaching methods to increase their understanding and love of learning? All systems merit this kind of analysis. For example, does a policy for ordering supplies get what is needed in time? Does a system designed to feed five hundred kids work for eight hundred? Is there a better way?

Stories About Continuous Improvement

Good, Better, Best
Complementary Angles

Sharing Power, Ownership, and Trust

It is the nature of a hierarchy to exert top-to-bottom control. Unfortunately, while the hierarchy gains accountability and authority, it also loses a great deal of effectiveness, efficiency, and spirit: Work is done for the boss, for the teacher, or for the superintendent, rather than for the real customer. Another approach suggests that when people own their work or their learning, together with a shared aim, they have greater interest, drive, and commitment. For this to happen, a supportive, nonthreatening, and trusting environment is necessary.

What are we saying to a teacher when a fifteen-dollar request for supplies requires five signatures? What are we saying to kids when we ask them to memorize facts with no sense of why the information is useful or important? What potential are we confining when we set limits and hold the power? On the other hand, what can students, teachers, and staff accomplish when they understand purpose and have what they need to do their best?

Stories About Power, Ownership, and Trust

Skippin' Out
The Notebook
Meeting Maggie's Needs
Wrestling Out a Budget
Kitchen Duty
TOPP Team
If Geese Can Do It
Complementary Angles

Encouraging Teamwork

Effective teams are stronger than the sum of the individuals. Yet many barriers to teamwork exist in organizations. Individual units or departments tend to develop policies and procedures that safeguard their own interests. A subculture emerges, often with its own norms, language, myths, and rites of passage. People are rewarded for doing their own work and ranked against their peers. But real improvement comes from improving systems and processes that cross individual and department lines. To do that, people need to be able to see beyond their organizational cubbyholes and be recognized for team gains.

Schools are no different. Teamwork among teachers, administrators, parents, and community contributes to student success. In addition, the concept of teamwork applies to students. Students can learn from each other. Barriers are erected when we say "do your own work" and rank students against each other. Effective team learning requires a culture of respect and trust and a system for effective interactions.

Stories About Teamwork

> The Notebook
> Wrestling Out a Budget
> Kitchen Duty
> Hunting for Worms
> TOPP Team
> If Geese Can Do It
> Complementary Angles

Making Systems and Processes Work Better

Improving a system means improving the whole. In a world of increasing complexity, the tendency is to tinker with the thousand and one details that can go wrong. This viewpoint is static and reactive. A more dynamic and proactive approach is to step back and scan the broad landscape, looking for interrelationships. Such interrelationships are processes—or a series of activities performed to achieve a specific outcome.

A school can be seen as a system: a teaching and learning system. The best way to improve teaching and learning, then, is to improve the processes that make up that system—the counseling process, for example. How can we describe, analyze, and improve counseling so that more students receive the kind of help they need, when they need it? Or with regard to the teacher-parent communication process, can communication activities be changed so that the outcome (teaching and learning) is improved?

Stories About Improving Systems and Processes

Kidgets

Skippin' Out

Meeting Maggie's Needs

Wrestling Out a Budget

Dropping Classes, Dropping Kids

Good, Better, Best

JJ

Complementary Angles

Using the Scientific Method to Make Decisions

Problem, solution, problem, solution. Next problem please. . . . Managing is often evaluated by how many problems you can find and fix—real fast. We do, redo, and clean up the doo doo. Are we fixing real problems, or are we fixing symptoms? Data and scientific methods can help ensure we are developing systems that work, not ones that repeatedly produce problems to be fixed and refixed. These methods get us to root causes. The result is a data-driven organization that is operated less by intuition, anecdote, hunch, and "that's the way we've always done it," and more by analytical rigor.

The question "How do you know that?" can readily be applied to many school situations. Does the gifted and talented program at this school really make a difference in terms of educational outcomes? Does the attendance policy lead to better attendance or worse? Does the class schedule make sense in terms of teaching and learning effectiveness? How do we know? How can we find out?

Stories About Scientific Decision Making

Why, Jimmy, Why?
Hunting for Worms
Dropping Classes, Dropping Kids
Making Small Problems Big
Butt, Butt, Butt. . .

Rethinking Ranking and Grading

As Dr. W. Edwards Deming says, "About half of any group will be below average." And who feels good about themselves when they have been labeled "below average," or even "average," for that matter? Isn't each human being valuable? What good can come from ranking or labeling people in such a way?

Grades and rankings are used to measure the product of each student's learning in relation to the others. So, even if everyone learns what is important, half will still be below average. What if the aim, instead, is to have all kids master important skills? And the measure is that they learn—and can demonstrate—all the skills? If that is the aim, then what useful purpose do ranking and grading serve in an educational environment?

Stories About Ranking and Grading

Kidgets

The Notebook

Not Yet

Tinosaurs

Will the Real Customer Please Stand Up?

I'm Not Okay, Or You're Not Okay

Understanding Variation

Even if we do the same thing the same way every time, the results will vary. If you drop the same marble from the same spot aiming at the same point one hundred times, it will land in a slightly different place each time. If your hand gets bumped, or the marble hits a rock, it might land far away. But mostly the marbles land in a common range. Likewise, the same person shooting a basket, taking a test, or doing an assignment will have results that vary a bit within a common range. Sometimes, however, they will be way off due to special, unusual causes.

What is important about variation is how we react to it. If most students fall within a common range of scores, it is meaningless to rank them within that range. If a few fall far out of a range, they may need special help. If a problem arises once, we shouldn't create rules and policies that apply to all. If the same problem arises regularly, we shouldn't deal with it case by case; we should adjust the process and get to the root cause.

Stories About Variation

Kidgets

Not Yet

Dropping Classes, Dropping Kids

Making Small Problems Big

I'm Not Okay, Or You're Not Okay

Promoting Pride in Work

Most people want to do good work, see how they fit in, and contribute in a meaningful way. People are motivated by pride in a job well done. This inherent desire is often stripped away by archaic rules, regulations, and a controlling hierarchy. The result is that organizations are often thickly populated with dispirited people—clock-watchers with just-get-by attitudes. A different approach suggests that organizations need to believe in their people, help them understand their roles and purposes in the organization, and give them what they need to be able to do their best work.

In education, this concept applies to administrators, teachers, staff, and students. Teachers who feel valued, understand the importance of their jobs, and have the freedom and tools needed to do them will be motivated and have a commitment to doing great work. Students who feel valued, understand the importance of learning and their role in it, and have the freedom and tools to learn will be motivated to excel.

Stories About Pride in Work

Kidgets
Skippin' Out
The Notebook

Not Yet

Kitchen Duty

Tinosaurs

Will the Real Customer Please Stand Up?

I'm Not Okay, Or You're Not Okay

Quality Concepts and Stories Matrix

	Developing a Customer Orientation	Aiming at a Clear Mission & Vision	Continuously Improving Everything We Do	Sharing Power, Ownership, & Trust
Kidgets		X		
Skippin' Out				X
The Notebook				X
Meeting Maggie's Needs	X		X	X
Wrestling Out a Budget				X
Not Yet		X		
Why, Jimmy, Why?				
Kitchen Duty	X	X		X
Edward Bear			X	
Hunting for Worms				
Dropping Classes, Dropping Kids				
TOPP Team				X
Making Small Problems Big	X			
Tinosaurs				
Will the Real Customer Please Stand Up?	X	X		
Good, Better, Best			X	
If Geese Can Do It		X		
I'm Not Okay, You're Not Okay				
Butt, Butt, Butt . . .				
JJ		X		
Complementary Angles		X	X	X

Encouraging Teamwork	Making Systems & Processes Work Better	Using the Scientific Method to Make Decisions	Rethinking Ranking & Grading	Understanding Variation	Promoting Pride in Work
			X	X	X
	X				X
X			X		X
	X				
X	X				
			X	X	X
		X			
X					X
X		X			
	X	X			X
X					
		X		X	
			X		X
	X		X		X
	X				
X					
			X	X	X
		X			
	X				
X					

A Story About Stories—Brother Rick

A friend of ours is a minister. Years ago, when he was first starting out in the ministering business, he was the pastor of a small congregation in the hills of western Tennessee. He saw himself as a theologian, in the process of getting his doctorate from Vanderbilt University, yet working with simple folks, many of whom could not read or write.

One Sunday, Matty Lou Bird came out of our friend's church, smiling as she always did. She was even smiling when she said, "Brother Rick, we just loves you to death. We just loves you to death. But we don't understand a word you say."

He took it well. He called a meeting of the church elders, determined to get to the bottom of the problem: "This is what Matty Lou Bird told me, and I'm real worried about it. What does it mean?" Joe Stanton, a long-standing elder, didn't beat around the bush—"Well, she's right, preacher. We don't understand what you're saying. We're simple folks. Just tell us a story."

Brother Rick was spending all this money and years of his life to get a great education, a Ph.D. in theology, and all they wanted him to do was tell stories?

For the next six months he did some of the most intense listening he had ever done in his life. He would sit on the porch of the general store every Saturday, in the heat and humidity, and just listen. He discovered that the local folk used stories to communicate. They didn't deal with issues straight on. They didn't come at things directly. They told stories: "You shoulda seen what ol' Duke did yesterday. . . ."

Like building a house, the process of story telling enabled them to lay a foundation, frame the topic of discussion, fashion a window to see the world, and provide all the trimming and details.

Brother Rick learned that if he was going to be an effective preacher, he had better become a storyteller, too. And, in time, he did—Ph.D. from Vanderbilt notwithstanding.

To this day, people in his former congregation come up to him and remind him of a story he once told—a story that touched them, that made them nod and say "amen." They can't repeat the title of the sermon or discuss how it relates to a particular passage from the bible, but they remember the story—they got the point.

Consider this book to be our own little store porch. Pull up a chair and give a good listen. We have a few simple stories to tell you about quality in education. No data. No research reports. No fancy talk here. Just tales, most of them true stories, about kids and teachers, cafeteria workers and principals—people who spend their days working, learning, and living in our schools.

We hope that you, like Brother Rick's congregation, will carry these stories around in your head for a really long time.

The Stories

Kidgets

In industry: If you want to improve the product, put your attention on the process whereby the product is made, not on inspection at the end of the line. In education: If you want to improve the student's achievements, put your attention on the teaching/learning process, not on the achievements in examination.

— Myron Tribus

James worked on a conveyor belt. He made and inspected widgets.

He worked at the end of the line where door handles were made for cars. His job was to do final assembly and inspect. Each day, about 450 door handles came to James. He knew his job well. He knew how to inspect carefully and test the handles to make sure they were made according to acceptable specifications. He measured and tested by weight. Any handle that didn't meet standards, he rejected. Those that were exceptional, he marked *exceptional*, and they were used on demonstration models.

He knew his job was important. He knew that customers expected quality and that a car wouldn't be a quality car if the door handle didn't work. And meeting the specifications was the way to ensure it worked.

He knew that about 16 percent of the handles wouldn't meet specifications and that about 10 percent would be exceptional. It was a guide his supervisor used to make sure that James was doing his job well. Not too many, not too few.

Each day James did his work, confident that he was producing quality handles for the customers.

He was confident even though he never actually saw the completed cars. He never saw how the handles worked in the end. He wasn't even sure how they were assembled to the cars. And he never saw a customer use one.

James also never saw the steps that occurred before a handle got to him. He didn't know what Hank, Ivan, and Elaine did in those steps. And he didn't know what caused the handles to be different sizes and strengths. He just assembled and inspected.

Then one day a new manager, Hannah, came to the company. She said, "What if all handles met specifications?"

James laughed. New manager. She didn't understand that if he passed all the handles, some of the car doors wouldn't work, and the customers would be mad and not buy their cars anymore.

"No," she explained. "We won't change the specifications. We'll improve the process so that all door handles meet specifications."

James couldn't do anything about that. The handles were nearly done when they came to him.

She explained that they would have to study the whole process of making the handles, from design through completion, step by step.

So Hank, Ivan, Elaine, James, and Hannah got together and worked on the whole process. They found out what steps in the process resulted in variation on the measures and strength. They made improvements and reduced the number of rejected handles to 0.2 percent.

Then they went back to work. This time they raised specifications. And the new aim was to try to make all handles exceptional.

A new aim. A new paradigm. A new car company.

§

Melanie was a high school teacher. Every year about 27 kids came through on her conveyor belt. Her job was to add knowledge and test the kids to make sure they met the minimum standards. Any student below minimum standards did not graduate. Any student who excelled was labeled *exceptional* and given honors and special recognition.

She knew her job well. She knew that society expected graduates to have a minimum standard of knowledge. And tests and grades were a way to ensure that.

She also knew that about 16 percent of the students in her school in any given year didn't make it and that about 10 percent were given honors.

This standard ensured that she was meeting expectations. Not too lenient, not too tough.

Melanie was confident she was doing her job to provide an educated society even though she never actually saw what happened to the kids who went on to college or who took jobs. She didn't really see how they integrated the knowledge into their lives and their work.

And she never saw the steps the kids went through before they got to her: at home, in elementary and middle schools, and in the other classes in high school. She didn't really see what contributed to each kid's different level of understanding and strengths.

Then one day a new principal arrived. He said, "What if all kids passed?"

Melanie laughed. It was an insult to education to pass some of these kids with the pathetic level of knowledge they had. They couldn't read or do simple math!

"No," he explained. "We won't change the expectations. We'll change the process so that all kids can meet the expectations."

Melanie couldn't do anything about that. There was too much that happened earlier over which she had no control.

§

But suppose, just suppose, that we could get together and develop a process that would result in all kids meeting expectations and graduating.

And suppose, just suppose, we could go on and develop a process in which all kids would accomplish what we now call *exceptional*.

A new aim. A look at education as a process. Identifying what contributes to the overall success of each child. Aiming at success for each kid. No kid "fails." No kid is "scrapped."

A new aim. A new paradigm. A new world. If we can do it for widgets, why not for kids?

Discussion Starters

Concepts: aiming at a clear mission and vision; making systems and processes work better; rethinking ranking and grading; understanding variation; and promoting pride in work.

What is the value of labeling on a curve? What is the harm?

What processes and systems make it possible for all students to succeed?

What changes are needed to make all students capable of succeeding in your school? your state? our nation?

How can we look at other stages of the process to evaluate which learning methods are most effective?

Skippin' Out

People get rewarded for conforming. No wonder we are on a decline.

— W. Edwards Deming

Dick Hendricks, the principal of John F. Kennedy High School, stepped into Andy Farmen's third-period art class. At first, no one noticed. The kids were scattered. A small clump was jabbering away in one corner, and a group of maybe four or five, with Andy at the center, was gathered against the back wall.

All the rest were self-absorbed, intent on their own work.

Dick edged forward. One student looked over her shoulder, and the principal used the opportunity to ask, "What are you working on?" and stand beside her, listening, for a moment.

He moved down a line of students, complimenting them, chatting away in soft tones, until he came to Andy's group. There, the students were silent and squinty-eyed, watching Andy demonstrate a scraping technique.

After a minute or two, Andy stood up, saying, "That's the easiest way to get the texture you need." He put down the tool he had been using and stepped back from the table just as the principal said, "This is really great work, Andy. Really good stuff."

Somewhat startled, Andy mumbled an awkward, "Thanks," as Dick continued to talk: "I'm sure your exhibits this year will be just as good as last year's. You know, we always get comments on the students' work that you show at the board of education offices. Just great. Oh, and that student…what was his name? Roberto?…being a junior and getting paid to paint murals. That's fantastic."

The compliments kept coming—fast and furious now, like the finale of a Fourth of July fireworks display—until Dick finally zeroed in and said, "Well, before I go, can I see you in your office?"

They walked to Andy's cluttered, art-strewn office. Inside, the principal quickly shifted the agenda: "We've got a problem."

Andy responded, "Yeah, sure, how can I help?"

"You've been observed leaving campus early. Now I know that your prep period is the last period of the day, but you need to stay a half hour after that—till 2:30. That's what the contract requires," the principal said.

Andy thought for a second and then shot back angrily, "I've been observed? By whom? Or have you seen me?"

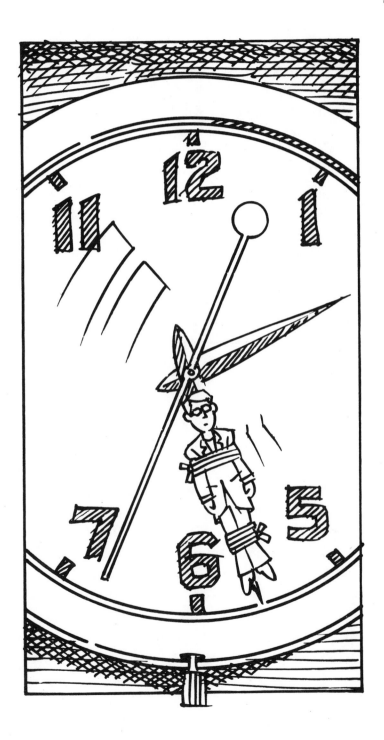

"No, no. I'm just making a statement. You've been observed leaving campus early."

Andy turned in his chair, his back to the principal, and looked out the window. His jaw tightened down, the muscles in his neck stiffened. Shaking his head in disbelief, his eyes happened to focus on the blue pickup truck in the parking lot. His car, the getaway vehicle.

He took several deep breaths trying to stay calm and then turned back to face the principal.

"Let me show you something, Dick." Andy grabbed an empty plastic bag off the corner of the desk. He pulled out a receipt for $8.25. "Yesterday I left a half-hour early to get several rolls of aluminum foil. We ran out. Without it, I would have fifteen or twenty students today on absolute shutdown. Then they get bored and cause trouble.

"You don't want bored kids, do you?" asked Andy.

"Of course not, Andy, I appreciate your willingness to spend your own money...."

Andy interrupted. "Then there was last week. Two days, Thursday and Friday, I left too. I was at a construction site, scrapping plywood, particle board, plaster, and silica sand. Those are all materials I use in class. I've lived here almost thirty years, Dick, and contractors, friends of mine, save stuff for me. I just have to get it."

"Look, Andy, I'm not trying to…"

"The week before I was at a photo lab. I made a deal with a former student of mine to process a double set of pictures that I take of the kids' projects. Now I can use one set for exhibits and send the other set home with the kids."

The principal stood up.

"Andy, your work is not the problem."

"Then what is?" Andy shot back. "Am I productive? How do you view me as a teacher?"

Dick half turned toward the door. "You're the best teacher in the art department. Everyone knows that. The kids love you. There's always a waiting list to get into your classes," he said.

"Well, then, stop right there. If I'm doing my job in the classroom, I don't think it's anyone's business what I do in my prep period."

"You don't understand, Andy," the principal said. "They're not my rules. I didn't negotiate them. I just live with them."

Andy looked straight ahead, his voice quivering ever so slightly: "So what's the bottom line, then?"

"The bottom line is that I want you to work to the contract time."

A student peered around the corner and said, "Mr. Hollinger? We're stuck."

Dick pushed through the open doorway.

And Andy mouthed the words, "Yes, sir," to no one in particular.

Discussion Starters

Concepts: sharing power, ownership, and trust; making systems and processes work better; and promoting pride in work.

How do rules and policies get in the way of a person's best efforts in your school?

How do they help?

Which rules and policies need changing or ignoring in your school?

Discuss how "class preparation" might be looked at as a process, not simply an act.

The Notebook

Joel is LD. That's *learning disabled.* Everyone knows that Joel is LD. So everyone tries to help Joel.

Joel's parents are attentive, caring parents. They are able to face the reality of Joel's disability and want to do everything they can to give him the extra help and support he needs to make his life successful.

He also has a good third-grade teacher who sees the value in creating the link with Joel's parents. She knows the link is important for any kid, and especially important given the extra barriers with which Joel has to deal.

So Joel's parents and his teacher got together and developed a plan. His parents initiated a notebook system. They asked his teacher to document Joel's activities each day. Then the parents would read it in the evening and know what to do to provide whatever support Joel needed for that day and for getting ready for tomorrow. Sounded good. Joel would carry the notebook back and forth, and the system was set.

Joel carried the notebook each day. He knew what the notebook was, just as he knew what LD was. The notebook was the report on him. It told about what he was doing that was different from other kids. It directed his life. His mom and dad asked each night for the notebook. His teacher asked each morning. Back and forth. The notebook owned power. Not Joel.

Joel began forgetting the notebook. And that made Mom and Dad unhappy. They wanted to do what was best for him and couldn't without the notebook. The notebook owned sharing. Not Joel.

His teacher became concerned that they wouldn't be able to provide the best learning conditions for him without the notebook. The notebook owned learning. Not Joel.

It seemed that Joel was being disobedient. Perhaps the lack of responsible remembering was another part of his "disability." Or perhaps, in this case, he was disabled by not being enabled.

Maybe the answer was in the notebook.

§

Joel's teacher and parents discussed Joel's behavior. They talked to Joel. They learned that Joel needed to own the sharing and the power. So they decided to let Joel own the notebook.

They gave the notebook to Joel and told him it was his. He made his own cover. Each day, it was his job to paste his work in the notebook. Beside each piece of work he would write what it was, how he did it, and how he felt about it. He showed each day's entries to his teacher, and she gave him encouragement and suggestions. She wrote her thoughts and comments in the notebook next to Joel's.

Each night he would carefully pack his notebook and take it home to his parents. He would explain each piece and tell stories about what he did and how he did it. His parents had a special place in the notebook to add their comments.

Each morning he would take the notebook back to his class and add a new day's work.

Joel now owned a part of the process of his own learning and development—a part he carried inside himself.

Discussion Starters

Concepts: sharing power, ownership, and trust; encouraging teamwork; rethinking ranking and grading; and promoting pride in work.

In what ways do we empower and disempower students? How does our behavior affect their motivation and pride?

How can teachers, kids, and parents work together to aid the learning process?

Meeting Maggie's Needs

Our schools are still set up as though every mother were at home all day and the whole family needed the summer to get the crops in.

— Sidney Callahan

Maggie Brown got home at 4:30 from a long day as a hotel maid. Her work day had begun at 7:00 A.M. Her legs were pounding tired before she even began her mile walk home on a dark, cold night in Brooklyn. She could hear the younger kids fighting as she came up the stairs, but they stopped when she came in, and helped her with her bags and coat. Her fifteen-year-old son, Jamah, had made sandwiches and soup for the younger kids, and had kept some for his mom. He knew she had a meeting at 5:30, and she would have only a few minutes to eat and get ready.

Maggie quickly washed up and changed her clothes. Then she sat at the table, and the kids joined her. She asked each of them about their day at school. Martin was still full of wonder and loved third grade. He told about a science experiment they did that made this foaming stuff grow and grow and spill over the top of the jar and out over the table. Serena said she was going to run for student council. She wanted to buy poster boards and markers to make signs for her campaign.

Jamah was usually quiet, but more so lately. Maggie knew Jamah had great potential. She had listened to him talk in full sentences before he was two, and he seemed to teach himself to read. He had a special gift for math and approached difficult situations with calm logic. But lately, his grades were not the best, and his mind was full of distractions. She didn't know where to start to help him.

She worried about her kids walking to school past crack dealers and gangs. And she worried about being able to afford the equipment, the lessons, the clothes, and the materials it would take to enable them to take advantage of the opportunities that did present themselves.

Maggie finished her dinner, hugged the kids, and left to walk the ten blocks to the school meeting.

Twelve parents were there, three teachers, and the principal, Mr. Violetto. This night, Mr. Violetto explained that the school wanted to increase parent involvement. He knew how critical parent involvement was to the success of students. So the school wanted to learn how to involve them more. Previous efforts over the years had netted few parents. Not surprisingly. A survey of parents indicated that only 15 of 55 families who responded included two parents. And most of the families had multiple children with an average income of $10,000 to $20,000 per year. All these factors told the school administrators and teachers that it would be hard for these parents to make it to school meetings.

But they decided to try a new angle. They decided to ask parents what they needed. They decided to listen. And so, at this meeting, Mr. Violetto asked, "What do you and other parents need to be able to be more involved in the school?"

Maggie spoke first. "I'll tell you what I don't need, Mr. Violetto. I don't need you to tell me how to raise my kids like the last principal did." A mumbling of voices and nodding of heads indicated other parents agreed.

"We need to be able to meet at a later time. Most of us don't get home until at least 5:00," another parent said.

A man in the front row added, "Mondays are a problem because the middle schools meet that night, which forces us to choose between schools."

Suggestions were flying.

Maggie spoke again: "We want our kids to graduate and to have a future beyond high school. We want to help the school make that happen."

"We need to know more about what opportunities are out there so we can help our kids prepare," a woman said, as two other people raised their hands.

"And I want to know how I can get my GED so that I set a good example for my kids," a father said.

The evening continued with the most active dialogue Mr. Violetto and the teachers had ever gotten from a group of parents. They captured every comment and asked several questions to be sure they understood what they needed.

Then, Mr. Violetto decided it was time to demonstrate his intent. He said, "The next meeting will be at 6:30 on Wednesday. It will be held in the Career Advising Center, and one hour will be devoted to covering post–high school opportunities. We will include information on GED testing."

Thirty-six parents showed up at the meeting.

At each meeting, the administrators and teachers continued to listen to the parents who came. They did everything they could to meet their needs. They knew how hard it was for the parents to come, so they wanted to do whatever they could to make it easy and worthwhile.

Little by little, over the course of the school year, they began to see positive impact in some kids. More homework was done on time. Kids came to the Career Advising Center and asked more questions. Parents made calls and sent notes to teachers about significant developments in their children's lives.

Meanwhile, the attendance at the parents' meetings continued to grow. The parents began to talk about how they thought their membership dues should be spent. They decided to sponsor a family night of eating, sharing, and singing together to strengthen their community. Four hundred parents, kids, and teachers showed up. The parents then helped set up partnerships with local businesses to expose kids to real jobs. Jamah visited a computer firm and became interested in their research and development.

The parents had more ideas, but they decided that their current dues amount would not be sufficient to accomplish them. So they voted overwhelmingly to triple their dues.

At Maggie's first meeting, only 12 parents had shown up. At the meeting nine months later, 211 parents came.

Discussion Starters

Concepts: developing a customer orientation; continuously improving everything we do; sharing power, ownership, and trust; and making systems and processes work better.

Are parents treated like customers in your school? Do you know what they need to become involved? How can you learn more?

What processes and systems enable contributions by parents?

What can you empower parents to do?

Wrestling Out a Budget

Things which matter most must never be at the mercy of things which matter least.

—Goethe

Greg is a high school wrestling coach in a small school in the Midwest. Although he had been an assistant coach for a few years, this was his first year as a head coach, and with the title came new responsibilities. Among them, the annual budget.

The paperwork arrived on his desk one day in late March. The forms had few instructions. He had no idea what the limits were and didn't know whom to ask.

So he looked at last year's budget. He carried over the travel expenses for "away" matches and added some funds to replace a few worn-out uniforms. Then he looked through the wrestling supply catalogs. He found a whistle for $12 to replace the broken one he used constantly for practices.

He needed stopwatches. He requested two for $22 each. He found harnesses to use in practice to

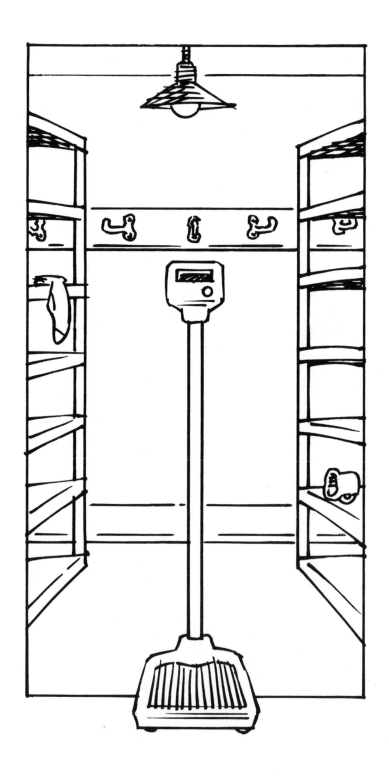

teach the kids to keep their arms close to their bodies. They cost $45; again, he requested two.

Then he saw an electronic scale. The manual scale they had was heavy and a bit of a hassle. It would do; but the electronic scale would be help-ful—if there were funds to pay for it. It cost $400. He submitted his budget.

A few weeks later, the return paperwork arrived:

whistle	$12	denied
stopwatches	$44	denied
harnesses	$90	denied
electronic scale	$400	approved

No one had talked to Greg about the budget. He didn't know who made the decisions. He asked someone in the superintendent's office if he could take the $400 for the scale and use it on the other items instead. He couldn't. They didn't say why. He would need to buy the whistle and stopwatches with his own money because he needed them to do his job.

If someone had talked to Greg or asked him his priorities, he and the wrestlers would have got-ten what they needed, and the school and the tax-payers would have spent less. Everyone would have won. Instead, no one did.

Incidentally, the same invisible person who made the decision about the wrestling budget also decided about the budgets for art, music, biology, geography, cleaning supplies, and the nurses' station.

Discussion Starters

Concepts: sharing power, ownership, and trust; encouraging teamwork; and making systems and processes work better.

In what ways do we empower and disempower teachers?

What are the processes for decision making in your school system? Do the processes put the decision-making power with those people who best know the needs?

Can you envision a way to develop a sense of teamwork between the budget maker and the budget user?

Not Yet

There are no grades, no incompletes, no Fs. The task is not complete until the work is perfect. The students have defined perfection for themselves and, therefore, know how to aim for it.

— Mt. Edgecumbe High School, Sitka, Alaska

K ris and Jolita had been buddies from grade school through middle school, and now they were starting high school together. They had learned their own way of getting by in school. They knew how to find out what the teachers expected, what they would accept, and how to get Ds, good enough to barely pass, without an extra ounce of work. They headed straight to the back of every class where they could hunker down and zone out.

Mr. Opheim was their high school homeroom teacher. He explained to the class that this school had a different system for measuring learning. There were standards of skills and knowledge that each person would be expected to master. Moreover, there were no Ds or Fs. If you didn't master the learning, you would get an NY, meaning *not yet*, and be given more time and help until you learned it.

Kris and Jolita didn't really listen or understand. They proceeded through the semester as always. Periodically, their teachers reminded them that they were expected to master certain knowledge. But they had already mastered their own system of getting by. Their interim scores were low, and again teachers reminded them of the standards and gave them alternative methods for catching up. But they continued to slide by with what they had learned as acceptable. Until...report card time.

Kris and Jolita got NYs in science.

They asked what an NY was.

Mr. Opheim explained it again. He said that they had not mastered the level of knowledge that was expected and needed to move on to the next level. It meant they would have to go to classes after school, on Saturdays, and/or during breaks until they mastered those skills.

Ahhhh! Horror of horrors! How could they do this? It was a dirty trick. The expectations had changed, and that wasn't fair. They had earned their Ds, and they deserved to get them and be allowed to move on.

Jolita was especially angry. She went to the assistant principal, Mr. Jenkins, and threatened to have her parents call.

Mr. Jenkins told Jolita he knew she could do better, and he expected it. Back to the books.

Kris and Jolita went to special sessions. The teachers offered them some alternative learning methods, including reading and outlining, cooperative groups, or demonstrative experiments.

Begrudgingly, Jolita chose a group. She thought she could get others to do the work and still get the credit. The team started to develop a science project, and Jolita sat back. She wasn't going to let them trap her into this. Besides, she was a bit worried. She didn't know if she *could* do the work. She'd never really tried.

Mr. Jenkins said he knew she could do it, but how the heck did he know? What if she couldn't? She preferred to think she could do it if she wanted to rather than to risk failure.

She sat back and watched, session after session. She began to realize that she understood what was going on. One day, as she watched the team proceed, she noticed they had the measurements wrong, so she corrected them. And then she noticed a better way to set up the equipment so the chemical activity was more visible. As the students discussed the results, she realized she understood everything they talked about. In fact, she had a few observations of her own, so she added them.

For the next experiment she really wanted to try the one where they were asked to separate compounds into basic elements by using heat and cold. She argued for it and agreed to do most of the setup if they chose that one. When they did choose it, she worked for three nights to help do the experiment, and she set aside a Saturday morning to help write it. She even asked her teacher to help her create special charts on the computer to use in the report.

Jolita was busy wondering what experiments they would be doing next when she was handed their report. The team had passed and received a B.

As the bell rang, Jolita jumped from her seat and ran out of the classroom. She almost bumped into Mr. Jenkins in the hall.

"Mr. Jenkins," she said. "I got an honest-to-God B!"

She smiled at the sound of her own voice and headed to her next class. On her way, she pondered her new feelings. She had learned something about science, and she liked it. And somewhere, deep down, she felt a new sense of who she was and what she might be capable of doing. And it felt good.

Discussion Starters

Concepts: aiming at a clear mission and vision; rethinking ranking and grading; understanding variation; and promoting pride in work.

How would a "Not Yet" approach affect the way you work at your school?

Discuss the process and impact of introducing outcome-based education when students are used to traditional methods.

Discuss how expectations can influence performance.

Why, Jimmy, Why?

I began to make my mind work the way theirs did. I spent my evenings with my eyes shut and my body wiggling the way Joe's did. I'd hear people talking to me and immediately forget what they had said the way Samantha did. Instead of bringing cumulative folders home in my briefcase each night, I carried a different child home in my heart.

— Dawna Markova in *How Your Child* Is *Smart*

He had enrolled late—a frail-looking, rough-around-the-edges boy named Jimmy. As his teacher, Steve Wachsman, hunted for a chair, Jimmy stood in the back of the art studio with a bored, stubborn look on his face.

"Jimmy, why don't you sit over here," Steve said.

Jimmy didn't move. He didn't even acknowledge that Steve had spoken to him.

"Jimmy?" he repeated.

Still nothing.

Steve walked to the back of the class and said to him, "There's your seat. Would you like to sit down?"

"No. I'll stand. You're telling me what to do already. Just leave me alone. Okay?"

This was exactly what he needed, Steve thought. The class was full, and he had to put up with some wise-cracking punk of a kid. He should tell the assistant principal to make him someone else's problem. He had his quota already. But where did that stiletto-like tongue come from anyway? "I'll stand . . . just leave me alone." Why would he say that?

Why?

Steve managed to corral Jimmy in his office at the end of the class. He tried to get an answer. It didn't take Steve long to figure out that Jimmy resented authority in a big way. It wasn't him. It was what he represented.

Why?

The next day Steve got a chance to talk to Jody Krall, the school's guidance counselor. He found out that Jimmy had been through juvenile hall. He had been caught stealing things from stores and then selling them for cash.

Why?

Later in the week Steve announced that a $10 fee would be collected the following Monday. The fee was for art supplies. Most of the students were aware that there was a class fee. Jimmy's face, however, registered this amused look as if to say, "Why not make it a thousand?"

After class, Steve spoke to Jimmy: "Is there a problem?"

"I don't have the money. That's the problem," he shot back.

"Well, can your parents pay it?"

Jimmy said, "They're not my parents. And they won't give me money for stuff like this. They don't trust me."

Why?

The following day Steve called Jimmy's home. He explained the situation to the mother. She said, "We're Jimmy's foster parents. He's having a lot of troubles. We're trying, but sometimes we just don't know what to do. We've punished him and restricted him, but it doesn't seem to make much difference."

Why?

"Well, I guess he's just a tough nut," she said. "He's had to be. Not many kids have lived in eight different foster homes from New York to California."

Discussion Starters

Concept: using the scientific method to make decisions.

What problems are you dealing with right now in your school?

How much do you really know about the circumstances surrounding these problems?

What are the root causes? Continue to ask "why" several times—like peeling an onion—until you get deep into the problem.

Make a list of problems in your organization. Ask "why" five times about each one. You are likely to find the same few root causes appearing over and over.

Kitchen Duty

You can't run a school if the oil filters aren't changed on the busses. No one realizes how important their job is until it isn't done.

—A school maintenance mechanic

A series of unfortunate off-campus, lunchtime incidents had occurred at Las Portales High School—a fatal car accident, several arrests for drugs at a local hamburger stand, numerous complaints from neighbors about kids smoking on the street corners. The hue and cry from parents and politicians had reached fever pitch.

And so the local school board acted decisively.

On Monday morning Ernie Becerril, the principal, got the following official memorandum: "As of Monday, November 12, Las Portales High School will be a closed campus. Lunchtime will run from 11:30 until 12:05."

Monday! That's one week. Principal Becerril's eyes glazed over. Panic was the logical course of action. Or maybe a quick transfer. "Geez," he thought, "that's 2500 kids to feed in 35 minutes. We've fed 350 or 400 in an hour before, but . . . "

By Wednesday extra tables and chairs had arrived. A portable field kitchen provided temporary help on the cooking side. On Thursday morning a set of new digitized cash registers with on-line inventory control and cost accounting were hooked up. Later that afternoon the staff received an hour's worth of training. Additional supplies—utensils, plates, glasses, and so on—were delivered Friday.

Everything was ready to go.

But when the 12:05 bell rang on Monday afternoon, 600 or 700 kids were still waiting in line to eat.

While the life of a principal is full of surprises, many things are predictable; for example, when 600 or 700 kids don't get to eat, there is a very good chance the principal will receive a telephone call or two.

But rather than spend the afternoon making excuses, Dr. Becerril went down to the cafeteria and met with the kitchen workers. He let them complain that they still didn't have enough tables, or enough time, and that the new cash registers were just too complicated. The complaint list was long.

Then he asked: "Why are you here? What do you believe about the young people who come here every day?" These were certainly not the kinds of questions that cafeteria workers were usually asked. After a long silence and a few false starts, a twenty-year cafeteria veteran piped up and said, "We're here to feed these kids. We're here to make sure they get a decent meal so they can learn."

The principal responded, "Then I believe what you believe. I'll be down here tomorrow at 10:30, and we'll do whatever we have to do to make sure they get fed."

And there he was on Tuesday—plastic hat, apron, and gloves. Ready to go. Ready to get it done.

The bell rang at 11:30. A blizzard ensued—cafeteria workers were flying around, dishes of potato salad and cartons of milk were scooped up and replaced, apples and pears were eaten on the run.

The bell rang at 12:05. No line. No students. Everyone had been fed.

How? How did they manage to do it? The workers began to gather around one of the cash registers where Dr. Becerril had been working. The cafeteria was a mess. Boxes had been torn open. Pans were lying around. And then there was the money. It was everywhere. They had figured out that knowing how to run the cash register had nothing to do with feeding the kids, so they didn't ring anything up. They just took money and made change.

But the kids—every last one of them—got fed.

Before leaving to go back to his office, Dr. Becerril asked the workers one more question: "Now, what do you need to do this every single day?

"You tell me what you need," he continued on. "And I'll try to get it for you."

Now the telephone calls came from the superintendent's office, not the parents: "What's going on down there? You're not using the new cash registers." To which his response was, "We can feed the kids, but we may or may not use your new cash registers. I'll just have to wait and see if the cafeteria workers want them."

§

Three days later the cafeteria supervisor called and said, "Doc, can you get us a few more hours of training on the registers. We need some square tables, too. All those round ones they sent us take up too much room."

Three weeks later she called again and said, "Doc, will you have someone come and get these registers?"

His first thought was, "Oh God, which ones?"

She continued, "We need to get rid of these old ones. They're in the way. We don't need them anymore."

Their decision. Not the principal's. Not the superintendent's.

With dignity and respect, he had challenged them to do an important job.

With trust and patience, he had enabled them to reach their own conclusions about how to get that important job done.

Discussion Starters

Concepts: developing a customer orientation; aiming at a clear mission and vision; sharing power, ownership, and trust; encouraging teamwork; and promoting pride in work.

What motivated the workers to try so hard?

Discuss the concept of shared mission (why we exist) and vision (what are we trying to accomplish?).

Think about all the jobs in your school and how each contributes to the mission of the school: educating kids. Does everyone understand the importance of their contribution to that mission? Do they know that the leaders appreciate their contribution?

Discuss the impact of this shared mission and vision on teamwork, continuous improvement, and promoting pride.

Edward Bear

The significant problems we face cannot be solved at the same level of thinking we were at when we created them.

— Albert Einstein

H ere is Edward Bear," Linda Marlin tells her cluster of cross-legged, wide-eyed kindergartners, "coming downstairs now, bump, bump, bump, on the back of his head, behind Christopher Robin."

Every time Linda reads *Winnie-the-Pooh*, the kids jump in right from the beginning. She pauses briefly after saying "coming downstairs now . . . ," and then the kids add the "bump, bump, bump."

They love sitting on the floor listening to— and occasionally joining in on—the stories about Pooh's adventure; Eeyore the old, grey donkey's birthday; and Piglet's encounter with a Heffalump. Linda sometimes thinks she knows the characters as well as she knows her own family.

"It is, as far as he knows, the only way of coming downstairs." Linda looks from one kid to the

next, pulling each youngster into the bumpy plight of Edward Bear.

§

Bump. How can you teach chemistry in thirty-seven minutes? Ginger Woolf has been frustrated by the scheduling at her junior high school. She can't really do any experiments in 37 minutes, but that is what she gets. It's what she has always gotten.

Bump. Pat Barton teaches ninth grade. The kids who come to him out of middle school are rarely prepared to do the work in his class. So every year he devotes the first month to review work and getting his kids up to speed.

Bump. Why does she bother? Karen Strong found a map for $22 advertised in a teacher's magazine. She knows it would be useful in her third-grade class. However, the school district's form requires four signatures and takes six to eight weeks to process. She isn't guessing. She knows. That's exactly what it took last year to get a map.

§

". . . but sometimes, he feels that there really is another way . . . " Linda continues, the kids hanging on every word of the story—"if only he could stop bumping for a moment and think of it."

Discussion Starters

Concept: continuously improving everything we do.

What are the "bumps" in your work?

Do you think there might be a better way?

Can you make improvements a step at a time?

Are there lessons to learn and data to collect while you are still bumping?

Hunting for Worms

Our third graders keep data on their spelling test. They experiment with different study techniques and chart their scores accordingly. Then they can see which study techniques are most effective for them.

— Theresa May Hicks, teacher

James Ellingson is standing on the lawn next to his school in Moorhead, Minnesota, on a lovely spring day. A 60' x 100' rectangle has been marked off. He is talking about protective coloration with his fourth-grade class.

"Imagine that robins are taking advantage of the spring weather to go hunting for worms and that we are the worms," he says.

"What color worm do you want to be?"

He begins to sprinkle "worms"—300 colored toothpicks—onto the rectangle. The toothpicks are red, blue, green, yellow, and natural. Sixty of each color. Like all good scientists, the students make predictions.

"I don't want to be red. That's for sure."

"If I was green, they'd never find me."

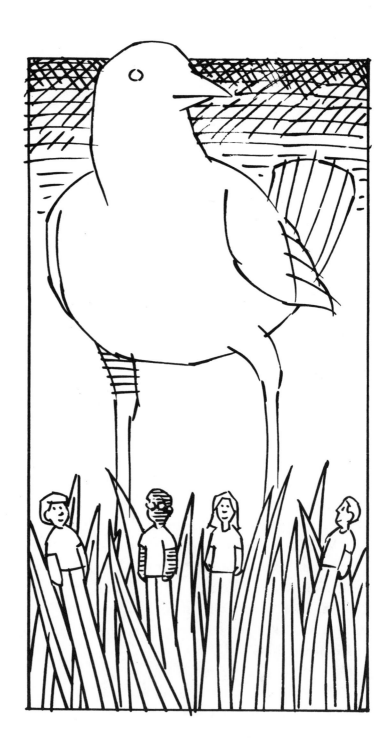

Eighteen kids collect data. They get down on their hands and knees and try to find as many toothpicks as they can. They count all the reds. Then the blues. When it comes to the greens, they find only seven of the 60.

To compare fractions, the students draw five columns—one for each color—and enter the appropriate numbers in each column. The numbers range from a low of 7 to a high of 56. Yellow worms are clearly a robin's feast.

The table enables the students to confirm or disconfirm their "worm hunting" hypotheses.

§

A scientific inquiry always follows the same process. First you frame the question: What color worm do you want to be? Then you make the hypotheses: Probably green or blue. You gather data: Counting toothpicks. And, finally, you formulate a fact-based conclusion: If you ever have to choose what color worm to be, choose green, not yellow.

Discussion Starters

Concepts: encouraging teamwork; using the scientific method to make decisions.

What are the steps in the scientific method?

How does this inquiry process help to improve quality?

"Counting worms" results in a checklist and then a table. What is the role of data in the inquiry process? Without it, how would the students respond to the question, "What color worm do you want to be?"

What are the most pressing issues in your job? What kind of data can you collect?

Dropping Classes, Dropping Kids

We learn best from our experience, but we never directly experience the consequences of many of our most important decisions.

— Peter Senge

Howard High was having a problem. Many kids were trying to drop or change classes. Two to six weeks into the semester, 200 kids out of a school of 2000 wanted to change or drop a class. Each change created confusion. In some classes, one or more students were gone all of a sudden. In other classes, the teachers had to quickly integrate new students into their classes. The paperwork was confusing, and if you got it mixed up, grades and credits were a mess.

So the administration dealt with the situation. The problem: too many kids wanted to drop or change classes. The solution: make it difficult to do.

They set up a review panel. To drop or change a class, you had to present your case to the panel.

The panel met at night, and you had to bring your parents. The panel consisted of teachers; they rotated duty.

When you appeared before the panel, they asked what your reasons were for wanting to drop or change classes.

The criteria for approving a drop were very limiting; few could meet them. You could not complain about a teacher. You could not complain about excessive workload. Although parents were required to be there, they were discouraged from participating. Students were expected to plead their own cases.

It worked! After only one semester, hardly any kids asked to drop or change classes. The problem was solved!

Wait. Let me see that problem again. Was that the problem? Or was that a symptom?

§

Sharon was a junior. She was a promising, college-bound student; high honor roll. As usual, she signed up for a full load of demanding courses. A week into the semester, she learned that she had an opportunity to take a college course. It was in biology, which was her chosen field. She was flattered to be chosen and excited about the challenge. But she had a full load of courses. She would have to drop a class to take the college course.

She appeared before the panel. Her case did not meet the criteria. No one had anticipated her situation, so the criteria for dropping did not include it as an allowable exception.

Case denied.

§

Susan was a freshman, college bound. She signed up for French I and knew she would need to take another year or two to be eligible for college. On the first day of class, the teacher handed the students a book and told them to study the first chapter. He spoke French exclusively during the rest of the class period. Susan had no idea what he said. The next two weeks were the same. At the end of the second week, he gave a test.

Susan didn't know what to study or how—and she got a D. She was worried. She was getting bad grades. She wasn't learning French. And how would she ever be able to take French II?

She appeared before the panel. She began to explain the problem, but a panel member cut her off when she started to complain about her teacher.

Case denied.

§

Jane, Rex, Jeff, and Kyle appeared that night, too. They all had the same French teacher as Susan. All denied.

§

Chris was a slide-along and do-only-what-you-have-to student. He signed up for the required courses, and he thought geography sounded cool, so he took it. After a few weeks he found out it wasn't as cool as he had thought—and it was hard work. So he wanted to drop it.

Chris appeared before the panel. He had friends who knew the criteria, so he knew how to present his case—though he had to stretch the truth beyond recognition.

Case approved.

Discussion Starters

Concepts: making systems and processes work better; using the scientific method to make decisions; and understanding variation.

What were some of the assumptions that went into designing the system for dropping classes? Were the assumptions based on data?

What was the problem(s)? How much did the administration know about the real problem?

What would happen if the administration had asked "why" a few times, as in "Why, Jimmy, Why?"

What were the effects of this process in the short run? In the long run?

What policies exist in your school? Are they accomplishing what they were intended to? How can you find out?

TOPP Team

I like to do math with a partner because then you have two brains working together.

— Melissa, third grader

Terry sat back in his chair and read the short memo one more time. It announced that Gail Burnham had resigned as principal. That was the fourth principal in six years. Quite a turnover. It was rotten for the school, but he couldn't blame Gail.

Ten years ago, Terry had come to Fairmount Middle School because of its progressive ideas about teaching. He was one of four teachers who taught fifth grade as a team.

Each teacher had one or two specialty areas. The kids changed classes during the day, going first to math and science, next to English, then to history, and so on.

Oscar, Paula, and Patricia were the other members on Terry's team. The four teachers met for 45 minutes every day to plan and coordinate their classes.

As Terry slid the memo into a pile of papers on his desk, he reflected on some of those meetings. The team members had been in charge of scheduling and curriculum, so they could coordinate the week and the subject matter as they wanted. Some of their best discussions involved when and how to introduce a topic so that the other teachers could build on it. He loved teaching that way.

The team also did the disciplining. Terry liked that because he quickly learned that the problems children had usually didn't occur as isolated events. As a team, the teachers could develop a coordinated strategy for Bobby or Lucas or whomever and, if necessary, call in the parents for a talk.

Terry really did enjoy Oscar and the gang. Four years they stayed together. They even had a name for themselves—TOPP Team—based on the first letters of their names. It was a lot of hard work and loads of fun.

We really did feel like we were the "topp," thought Terry.

Then, six years ago, the district had hired a new superintendent. The teams were dissolved, and everything returned to the old way. Terry, Oscar, Paula, and Patricia retreated to their adjoining caves, and each taught the same group of kids all day. They had no need for meeting and planning time. Lesson plans were submitted to the principal.

Discipline wasn't their responsibility any longer either. If a kid caused trouble, you just sent the little troublemaker to the principal's office.

Terry grabbed his coat.

Some days he really missed the TOPP Team. All his teammates had now left Fairmount Middle School. Oscar had a job in human resources with the telephone company. Paula had transferred to another school closer to her home. Patricia had gone back for her MBA and had been working at a bank for almost three years now.

There was a whole new batch of fifth- and sixth-grade teachers, but he rarely did much with them.

As he flipped off the light switch, Terry was hit by a wave of depression. He was so bored, so tired of the routine and the lack of challenge in his work. It wasn't much fun coming to work any-more; it hadn't been for years.

He walked by Gail's office and thought about sticking his head in—saying something, telling her he was sorry. But Terry knew that it was budget time, and Gail would be swamped. And besides, two sets of parents were waiting with their kids to see her—probably about the graffiti incident from earlier in the week. So he just dropped off his les-son plans for next week and headed to the parking lot.

Nope, he couldn't blame Gail.

While he was mostly underwhelmed by his job, she was completely overwhelmed by hers.

Discussion starters

Concepts: sharing power, ownership, and trust; encouraging teamwork.

What worked for the TOPP team? Why did it work so well?

Do teachers in your school have the opportunity to share ideas and work together in teams? Do they have the space, tools, time, and encouragement?

Are teachers in your school evaluated in a way that encourages or discourages sharing?

Why was Gail overwhelmed while Terry was underwhelmed? How are various responsibilities allocated in your school? Is there a better way?

Making Small Problems Big

Today's problems come from yesterday's solutions.

— Peter Senge

In Mr. Kipling's fifth-grade science class, five kids were behind in their work. Mr. Kipling contacted their parents and found they were willing to work with the kids. He sent home the textbooks with the children, along with special notes on what to cover. The kids progressed significantly in their work. As the year ended, Mr. Kipling reminded them to bring back the books. Three of them forgot.

Mr. Kipling had a thousand things to do and left the next week to spend the summer in Canada.

When school started again in the fall and it was time to hand out the science books, they didn't have enough. Mr. Kipling's former students had since moved on to middle school in another building, and Mr. Kipling was unable to recover all the books.

So, the school fixed the problem forever. It created a policy to apply to all cases: Books could not be taken home for extended use.

§

Jennifer finished first grade at an okay, but not so great, level. Her parents were educators and well aware of how important it was for Jennifer to keep up at this stage of her education. They wanted to work with Jennifer over the summer to help improve her reading skills, and they wanted to request Mr. Short for second grade. They knew Mr. Short's teaching style would be effective for Jennifer's learning style.

So, they called the school and asked to borrow some reading books.

The person at the school said she was sorry, but the school had a policy of not lending books for home use.

Jennifer's parents offered to pay for any books they did not return. The person said she would have to ask, since she didn't have the authority to interpret or change the policy.

They then asked about Mr. Short and were told that the school also had a policy that grouped kids in classes according to ability. The person said, "You can't have the books *and* Mr. Short: if you borrow the books, Jennifer will advance in her reading

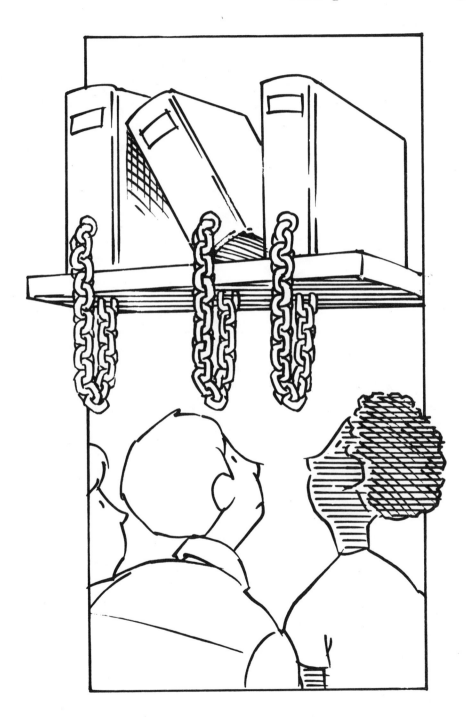

skills and be in the top reading group. And Mr. Short doesn't have the top reading group."

Their request for a teacher would have been okay, they were told, if Jennifer remained at her current, not-so-good reading level.

So the school's policies told them they couldn't use a book to help their daughter advance. And if they did, they would be punished by another policy.

§

Jennifer's parents were upset. They called the principal and complained. And then they complained to the superintendent.

That got action. The principal called them the following week to tell them it would be okay. They could have the books *and* Mr. Short.

Jennifer's dad asked how the school had rectified their concerns. The principal proudly explained that they had figured out a way to make it work. They simply moved all the kids so that Mr. Short had the top reading group.

And then lots of parents, kids, and teachers got mad.

§

Special, one-time problems got big-time solutions. And those big-time solutions created bigger-time problems.

Discussion Starters

Concepts: developing a customer orientation; using the scientific method to make decisions; and understanding variation.

The school made a policy regarding all books based on one incident. Then they moved all kids to address another isolated problem. What were the short-term effects of these decisions? the long-term effects?

What happens when we solve one-time problems with solutions that affect many? What decisions and policies do you have in your school that were made because of a single incident or problem?

How should we treat single incidents or problems?

Tinosaurs

The only legitimate purpose of an examination is to permit the teacher and learner to work together to decide how to improve the education process of the student. In other words, for the teacher and learner to decide what to do next.

— Reuven Feuerstein

Tony was an eager first grader. He had always been an enthusiastic learner. His mom often found him curled up with a book on a sunny afternoon. He was always asking questions. A trip to the grocery store, an hour in the garden, or a Sunday drive in the car would net new knowledge for Tony and for whoever shared his company. From his new knowledge, he would create stories and games and inventions and more questions.

Tony couldn't wait to go to school each day. He listened to every word his teacher said and always did more than he was expected to do.

One day his teacher read a story to the class about a dinosaur. Tony was fascinated. He went home and told his dad. They went to the library and checked out seven books on dinosaurs. Tony consumed the books, memorizing the dinosaurs'

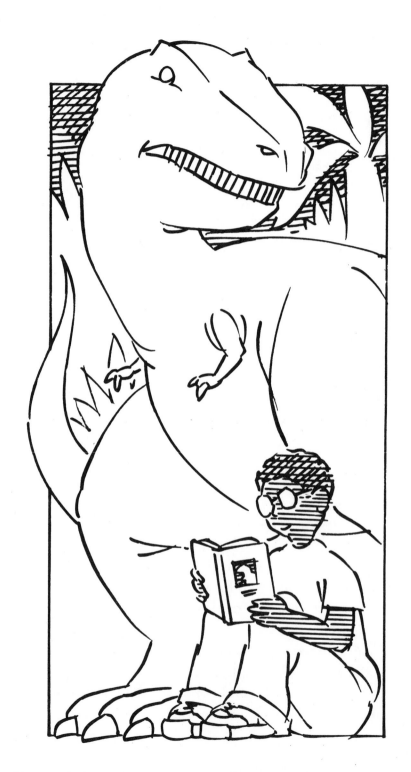

species, what they ate, and when they lived, and he began creating wonderful stories about dinosaurs.

In the meantime, back in school, they were learning about consonants. One worksheet had a picture of a dinosaur. The students were supposed to write the beginning sound in the blank below the picture. Tony wrote T. He got it wrong. He didn't get a star by his name on the board that day.

His mother was surprised. "Tony, you have been learning all about dinosaurs. How could you have gotten this one wrong?"

Tony answered, "I wasn't wrong, Mom."

"But Tony, *dinosaur* starts with a *d*. You know that."

"Mom, that's a Tyrannosaurus Rex."

Tony learned the right stuff wrong. Or was it the wrong stuff right? How can we measure "right" right and "wrong" right when wrong is sometimes right?

Discussion Starters

Concepts: rethinking ranking and grading; promoting pride in work.

How do we measure learning? What learning is hardest to measure?

What learning is most important?

What will Tony do now?

How can tests be most useful? How are they used in your school?

Will the Real Customer Please Stand Up?

Left to our own devices, we pay more and more attention to things of less and less importance to the customer.

— Tom Peters

Fred works in an appliance store. He sells appliances: washers, dryers, ranges, microwaves, and so on. People come to him to purchase an appliance for their homes.

Fred listens to their needs and tries to help them identify the best appliance to fit those needs. If they need a washing machine for their small apartment, he recommends the compact, stackable washer-dryer model. If they need a stove to cook for a large family and they don't have a gas hookup, he recommends a 36-inch electric range.

Sometimes the customers aren't very clear about their needs. They don't tell him they only have a 34-inch opening for the 36-inch range. Or they forget to mention that their washer will be used for heavy work clothes on a daily basis. Fred prides himself on asking the right questions. He has learned how to figure out what his customers really require.

Occasionally he finds he doesn't have what his customers need. Maybe he doesn't carry large ranges in the cost bracket the customers can afford. Or maybe they need a very special model, one that he doesn't carry. He tries hard to find a way to meet their needs.

He feels good when he makes a sale and great when he has found just the right appliance for a customer.

The product is the appliance. The measure of success is the sale. The aim is a good sales record and the knowledge that he has met his customers' expectations.

§

Mike is a seventh-grade student. He goes to his teachers to learn about various subjects: math, literature, history, social studies, science, art, and so on.

Mike listens to what his teachers want, and he tries to do his work to best meet their requests. If they want a short story with imagination, he tries to be imaginative. If they want a science project that uses 240 toothpicks, he uses 240 toothpicks.

Sometimes the teachers aren't very clear about what they want. They don't tell him he needs to use black pen on lined paper. Or they forget to mention that the toothpicks can't be plastic or the glue won't stick. Mike prides himself on his ability to find out just what the teachers want.

At times he finds he can't do what they're asking. Maybe he didn't understand last year's math to build on for this year. He tries to get as close as he can, but he worries that he hasn't done what the teachers expect. He doesn't want them to be angry or disappointed in him.

He feels good when he gets good grades because then his teachers are pleased.

The product is the test or homework. The measure is grades. The aim is to please his teachers and pass the classes.

But should it be?

§

Consider:

Gretchen is a seventh-grade teacher in another school. She teaches several classes of science. Students come to her for learning.

Gretchen listens to what their needs are and uses her expertise and training to find ways to best meet their learning needs. Adam learns best by being involved and doing experiments, so she offers those learning tools to him. Patty has gotten behind in her understanding of basic concepts, so Gretchen links her with a tutor to help her catch up.

Sometimes it's hard to tell what the students' needs are. She doesn't know about Sue's problems at home or that Mary's ear infection is affecting her concentration. But she prides herself on her ability to perceive and learn those needs.

Every so often she finds she doesn't really have what she needs to do her job. The equipment may be inadequate, or she may have more students than she can tend to. She works hard to provide the children with what they need for a successful life.

She feels good when students can demonstrate their learning, and she feels great when they enjoy learning and seek to learn more than she presents.

The product is learning. The measure is demonstrated understanding. The aim is to inspire children to engage in a process of lifelong discovery.

Discussion Starters

Concepts: developing a customer orientation; aiming at a clear mission and vision; rethinking ranking and grading; and promoting pride in work.

Who are the customers in your school? How can you tell?

Discuss the different missions and visions in this story and how they affect actions.

In Mike's school, the measure is grades. In Gretchen's school, the measure is demonstrated learning. What gets measured in your school?

Good, Better, Best

Being educated means to prefer the best not only to the worst but to the second best.

— William Lyon Phelps

The kids were lined up by the office. Some were there to be disciplined for fighting at recess. The others were there to have the school nurse fix their wounds.

Just like yesterday. Every day was like that. And it was worse when it rained.

What to do? The principal and teachers got together and began talking about adding another monitor, adding more rules. It sounded like more pain for everyone, but people seemed to agree that *something* had to be done. This solution was as good as any.

Good? Mary Ann Voss, a second-year kindergarten teacher, squirmed in her chair and fidgeted with the pencil in her hand. Something about the idea bothered her. Good? Is that it? Certainly they could do better than that.

Mary Ann couldn't shake the little rhyme in her head. It was one that she taught her students:

Good, better, best,
never let it rest,
till your good is better
and your better best.

She taught her kids that good just wasn't good enough—always strive to do even better, to do your best.

So, with no small amount of fear in her heart and with a slight quiver in her voice, she spoke: "I think the reason that there is so much trouble at recess is that the kids have nothing to do. Especially when it rains. The ground by the play equipment gets muddy and stays that way for days."

A few people agreed. Then a few more. It wouldn't be that difficult to install drains and new ground material by the equipment. Perhaps it would be worth a try before going through the trouble of hiring the additional monitor.

Better? Maybe so. But Mary Ann also knew that even when it didn't rain there wasn't enough playground equipment or space to accommodate 500 kids.

With a steadier voice this time, she explained the situation as she saw it: There wasn't enough equipment or space, really. Again, to her delight, the teachers seemed to agree.

Then the principal jerked them back to reality: "That's great, but there's no money in the budget for equipment."

Mary Ann responded, "Well, I wasn't really thinking about more equipment. Couldn't we stagger the recess times instead?"

Suddenly there was less all-for-one, let's-do-it-for-the-kids unanimity. A succession of doubters surfaced. "We've always had recesses at those times." "Those are the best times." "Who would have to change?"

So it took a bit of time for the dust to settle, but in the end, most people agreed that staggering the recess times was a possibility. And, along with the new drains and ground material, they agreed it was the best idea.

From rhymes to recess, it really does make sense not to settle for simple, quick-fix solutions, thought Mary Ann: "Good, better, best, never let it rest,..."

Discussion Starters

Concepts: continuously improving everything we do; making systems and processes work better.

What approach was used to address this problem? How did it help?

Discuss the policies, requirements, and procedures in your school. Ask yourself why they exist.

How might you identify old rules that need to be changed?

How might you do this on an ongoing basis—a system for continuously improving?

If Geese Can Do It

This is the true joy in life, the being used for a purpose recognized by yourself as a mighty one. . . . The being a force of nature instead of a feverish, selfish little clod of ailments and grievances complaining that the world will not devote itself to making you happy.

— George Bernard Shaw

The meeting seemed to be going nowhere fast. Maria Tellez, the superintendent of schools, had worked with a task force of teachers and administrators in drafting a strategic plan. Today she was presenting the plan to an audience of students, staff, parents, and community members.

The planning initiative had come in response to concerns expressed by the board of education. Even six months ago, when Maria was interviewing for the position, the board president had made it pretty clear that he perceived the school district to be adrift—no leadership, no direction, no purpose.

She had thought long and hard about taking the job. This would be her first superintendency, and she was under no illusions when it came to the amount of time the job would consume. As a principal she had still been able to teach biology and continue her lifelong interest in genetic coding and migratory patterns of birds. Ornithology was her true love.

But becoming a superintendent was something she wanted to do. So, she took the job.

Now she was having doubts. After each aspect of the strategic planning effort was presented, a steady stream of nay-saying followed. For example, an initial set of beliefs was read: "Our mission statement serves to keep our large, complex organization focused on our goals," and "We control the critical elements to guarantee success."

While most people agreed that focusing on goals was important, the staff members resisted the idea that they had any control whatsoever. Some argued that recent budget cuts guaranteed failure, not success; others insisted that state regulations tied their hands. In effect, goals were good, but no one could really be responsible for meeting them.

They expressed no sense of community or direction.

As each goose flaps its wings, it creates an "uplift" for the bird following. By flying in a "V" formation, the whole flock adds 71 percent greater flying range than if the bird flew alone.

As the debate continued into its second hour, Dr. Tellez began to feel the effects of the weeks of hard work. No one on the task force had felt

enthused about the planning effort. They had shown no sense of urgency either. The status quo lay across the group like a heavy blanket. Every excuse in the world existed to avoid making changes or difficult choices. "If it ain't broke, why fix it?" seemed to be the motto.

And so, Dr. Tellez had done 90 percent of the task force's work by herself. She had done most of the research and all of the writing. She was now presenting the plan.

She had done it all.

When the lead goose gets tired, it rotates back into the flying formation and another goose flies at the point position.

The meeting dragged on. Nothing seemed to be working. She could understand how some people could disagree with some proposals, but the bickering was nonstop. It was one thing to defend your school or your classes. It was something else to denigrate her efforts to improve the school district.

One person said, "This whole thing is a waste of time." Others nodded, and a third added, "This is just the latest gimmick to get teachers to do more and pay them less."

So, why bother?

The geese in formation honk from behind to encourage those up front to keep up their speed.

Dr. Tellez tried to explain to the audience how important the exercise was. "We can quibble over the details all we want," she said. "But the fact is, something needs to be done. We are facing some tough times ahead—budget problems, enrollment problems—and we really need to start pulling together as a community.

"This school district is in trouble."

When a goose gets sick, wounded, or shot, two geese drop out of formation and follow it down to help and protect it. They stay with it until it is able to fly again or it dies. Then they launch out on their own, with another formation, or catch up with the flock.

As the meeting broke up, Dr. Tellez sank heavily into her chair and wondered where she would find the energy to make this journey on her own.

Discussion Starters

Concepts: aiming at a clear mission and vision; sharing power, ownership, and trust; and encouraging teamwork.

Does everyone at your school or in your school district have a clear understanding of the vision—of where they are flying?

Do they use the same words when describing that vision?

How do you create a shared vision?

Does the lead goose at your institution seek support, nurture trust, and ensure that everyone owns the vision?

Are people willing to take risks to contribute to that vision and make it happen?

I'm Not Okay, or
You're Not Okay

I watch some kids in school who try as hard as they can and they still get Cs and Ds. And some kids who hardly try, and they always get As. It doesn't seem fair to those kids who try hard. It seems it's telling them they can't ever be good enough.

— Adam Cotter, sixth grader

S teve was excited about starting school. He loved to learn. As a baby he would study a toy for hours, turning it, tossing it, squeezing it, chewing on it. At four, he took apart the baby's swing and put it back together using his dad's tools. It was a bit lopsided after that, but Steve was sure his baby sister was getting a better ride.

Steve's parents were very proud of him. They supported and encouraged his learning, taking him to science museums, letting him use tools on real things (within limits), and answering his never-ending questions.

In kindergarten he was always the first to finish the hardest puzzles. He figured out the mental problems before anyone else understood the question.

They just seemed to click in his mind. And the learning games on the class computer were fascinating for him. He would just work the keys, turning the problems around and around, and the answers would seem to pop out. It was the active learning he enjoyed so much—doing things, making stuff work out.

Steve skipped off to the first day of first grade with the same enthusiasm. He had his own desk! He got busy setting it up with his brand new notebooks, crayons, ruler, dinosaur eraser, and squeeze bottle of glue. Ready to go. Ready to learn more.

He wanted to do well. So he sat as still as he could.

But his legs seemed to want to walk away. They would jump around and itch, and his arms would reach and stretch. His teacher asked him to please sit still and not distract the others.

She passed around work sheets and asked the students to print all the letters in the right spaces, as neatly as possible. They would be graded on their neatness and their ability to follow instructions exactly.

Steve worked very hard. His letters were awkward looking. He erased them and tried again. Each time he erased, his paper looked worse. And his hands got harder to control. An intense feeling of frustration welled up inside him, and he wanted to smash his pencil through his desk. He wanted to run down the hallways, to let his legs and arms stretch and pump.

When the class finished the sheet, Steve sighed and got ready to get up. But the teacher handed out another work sheet. The students sat at their desks for two whole hours before they went to recess that day. After lunch, they moved into work groups for awhile, but they stayed at their desks most of that day. And the next day. And the next.

§

Gloria was Steve's teacher. It was her third year teaching first grade. She viewed first grade as a formative year—laying a foundation for all the school years ahead. In first grade you learn to read. You learn basic math. You are a real student for the first time.

She knew it was an adjustment for kids who were used to less structure. But they would have to adapt if they were going to make it in school. Discipline was necessary in body and mind if they were to learn to read, write, and do math. So she was precise and firm, and she set the expectations clearly at the beginning.

She graded the first papers to set the tone. She wanted the students to know what was important and what level of work she expected.

§

Steve got the first work sheets back. They had a lot of red on them. Red felt-tip pen that didn't erase when he made the changes. The red showed how his letters were supposed to look and where

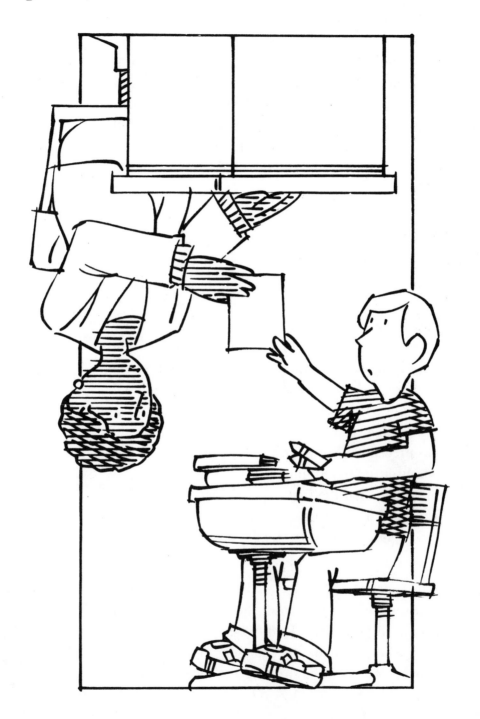

he had gone "out of bounds." He didn't want to take his paper home to his parents, so he crumpled it up and left it in his locker.

The second week Gloria had each child read to her individually. In the third week she announced the reading groups. Jamie and Sally, Steve's best friends, were put in the red group. Steve was in the blue group. Steve liked the kids in his group, and he liked the stories. But he could see right away that the red group was for smarter kids. At least he wasn't in the "dumb" group. He wondered what it all meant.

They started having timed tests on their math facts. Steve knew the answers, but his pencil wouldn't go as fast as his mind. His paper was an absolute mess, and he got some marked wrong just because the teacher couldn't read the answers.

Then his first report card came. Steve got a *satisfactory* in all areas. Jamie got four *outstanding*s, and Sally got five.

Steve was confused. His parents were concerned. They asked whether he was trying hard.

At conferences, Gloria told Steve's parents that Steve seemed to be bright but that he needed to be more careful with his work. And he needed to learn to sit still.

So Steve tried even harder. He gave up spending extra time on the things he enjoyed learning and tried to focus on doing a good job on those things his teacher wanted him to improve.

His second report card was the same.

Steve was mixed up. Thoughts ran around and around. Maybe he wasn't as smart as he believed. His parents thought he was smart. And now he was disappointing them. Maybe the teacher was wrong. Maybe the whole school was wrong. Maybe they didn't really know anything about him.

Steve was struggling with two thoughts, and it seemed that only one could be true. Either he was not as smart as he thought he was, or the teacher and the school were wrong.

If he believed the school was wrong, at least then he could believe in himself.

Discussion Starters

Concepts: rethinking ranking and grading; understanding variation; and promoting pride in work.

How is Steve being measured? Is that an accurate measure?

If it is true that Steve isn't as smart as some other kids, what is the value in identifying that? What is the harm?

Does Steve have a specific learning style? Talk about variety in learning styles. How does the typical classroom experience help or hinder different styles?

Steve had to decide who was okay. Discuss the consequences of either choice.

Butt, Butt, Butt . . .

It's a good idea if you don't think about it.

— Dagwood Bumstead

Data can sometimes take unusual forms....
"It's a state law: No smoking on school grounds," proclaimed the principal. "We don't have a choice. We have to find a way to stop the kids from smoking." The teachers and staff knew they had their work cut out for them.

In nice weather, the kids went across the street to smoke during recess and lunch hour. That made the neighbors mad.

But worse than that was during bad weather. They smoked in the bathrooms.

All you had to do was walk past the boys' bathroom. The smoke billowed out into the hall. And in the urinal lay dozens of disgusting butts. No question. It had to be dealt with.

"Let's brainstorm some solutions," they said.

"Teacher duty." They could take turns at the worst job in the school—monitoring the rest rooms.

"Cut out all student hall passes."

"Don't let anyone go to the bathroom during classes." We can keep an eye on them that way.

"Install smoke detectors that set off a sprinkler system. Getting rained on a few times might dampen the craving."

"Wait a minute. What do we really know about this problem?" one teacher asked. "Let's collect some data."

Data, in this case, consisted of butts.

So they set up a schedule. They collected butts in the morning right before classes, before and after morning break, before and after each lunch section, and at the end of the day.

The first thing they learned was that the custodian had gotten disgusted with the problem and had quit cleaning up the butts in the urinals. So the pile of disgusting butts they found on their first inspection did not represent one day's but several.

As they collected data, or butts, over the next few days, they learned more.

They found six butts in the morning, six butts after morning break, and six butts after second lunch session.

So then they watched. And they learned more.

Six boys hung out together. They usually entered the bathroom at the same time. And they exited at about the same time—about seven minutes later—with smoke tending to billow out about then.

The problem suddenly looked different.

And so did the potential solutions . . . for putting an end to the butts.

Discussion Starters

Concepts: using the scientific method to make decisions.

What decisions are made in your school without adequate data?

What data might be useful? How might data change the view of those problems—and of the potential solutions?

JJ

JJ, where you been, girl?" yells Rhonda from across the street as she dodges between the cars.

Turning to the sound of the voice, JJ recognizes her best friend. With the screech of brakes still hanging in the air, Rhonda hops up onto the curb.

"It's been a week. No—more. I called your apartment—phone's disconnected. What's the story? What gives?"

"Crap. It's just been crap," JJ almost screams. "They suspended me. Jus' can't believe it. I could graduate in a year, and they suspend me."

"Why? What for?"

"Attendance. If you miss one day, it's this. Two days, it's that." JJ spits out the words. "Five days, you get a week's suspension. Ten and you're out for good."

Rhonda jumps in. "But where were you?"

"Findin' a place to live. I went to the apartment the other week, and there was an eviction notice. Door locked. Furniture in the hall."

"Where were Bobby and your mother? Where was Michael?"

"Gone. She left with Bobby. That's what the lady next door says. Soon as the eviction men threw them out. She got some clothes and they left," JJ says, sort of matter-of-factly.

She starts walking faster, moving down the sidewalk in front of the school with Rhonda trying to keep up.

JJ still talking: "Michael's with me. He's OK. I looked for a place when he was in school."

"How'd you pay?"

"Got a job . . . working in that cleaner on the corner of Fillmore."

"Can't believe they left. I never liked that Bobby. He's scum," Rhonda jerks her head from side to side in frustration. "So, why you here?" she continues.

They stop at the corner. The light is red.

JJ turns. "I told you. Gettin' back into school. But they wouldn't let me."

"You told them, didn't you? Told them about Bobby and the job?"

"Yeah. There were whole bunches of people in there. Waited for an hour. So the man reads from this computer paper. You missed eighteen days, he says. Then looks on this other paper. Says to me—you're suspended. Get off the school property."

"They ain't nothin' you can do?" Rhonda asks.

"Oh yeah," JJ waves a crumpled piece of paper. "I can call tomorrow for an appointment. That's good. Got no phone."

"Appointment for what?"

"An appeal. I can bring in my parents. Hell. Her and Bobby are in Houston by now. Or something about a group or board. Meets Wednesday nights. I work nights."

Rhonda says, "That's it?"

"Yup. I started laughing. The man says I should have more respect. If I had more respect, I wouldn't be in this fix, he tells me."

The cars thin out. JJ runs across the street, arms pumping, hair flying. "Gotta pick up Michael from school," she yells over her shoulder.

"JJ, talk to Doc Braggs. He'll help," Rhonda yells back.

§

"Last order of business, people." Dr. Donald Braggs, principal of Carver High School, announced to the gathering of 50 or 60 teachers.

"I'd like you to take a moment and review our attendance policy. Two years ago we revised it. I thought we should ask ourselves how it's working."

A hand shot up immediately. "I think it's helped. Kids know that we have strict guidelines and that there are consequences."

"I agree," someone else said. "Parents know it too. When a student gets suspended for a week—they notice."

Another person had a different opinion: "Have you looked at it? It's seven pages long. It's too complicated—appeals and boards and forms."

"Well, I want kids in class that want to be there," a teacher in the back row responded. "I think it's too lax. There's too much slack. Kick them out after five absences, and make them request readmittance. Make them more accountable."

The discussion went back and forth for 15 minutes until Dr. Braggs cut it off.

"I think we missed the point on this," he said. "I think maybe policies have become more important than people. Some of you know JJ Matthews. She hasn't been in classes for a couple of weeks, and now she's suspended—indefinitely, I believe."

"I've invited her to join us," he said as he opened a door to the hallway.

JJ was uncomfortable and terribly self-conscious as she walked in with all those faces staring at her.

"JJ, tell us why you missed school."

She was embarrassed. But she did what Doc Braggs had told her to do: "JJ, just tell the story like you would tell it to your best friend." So she

did. She pretended she was on the street corner with Rhonda.

When she finished, there was silence. A few people shifted in their chairs.

Then Dr. Braggs spoke: "I know it's our policy. We make the rules—all seven pages worth. But *you'll* have to tell her she doesn't belong here. I can't."

Discussion Starters

Concepts: developing a customer orientation; making systems and processes work better.

What policies and procedures does your school have for guiding attendance and behavior?

How can you ensure that the policies and procedures aren't more important than the kids? How can you know?

Complementary Angles

The definition of education is to learn from within ourselves. Quality methods provide a bridge for communications between students. When communication is good, we can be real open with those we are working with. Then we can learn from inside of one another.

— Keyur Parikh, high school junior

Nicolo LaMasa finished advanced English, his last class of the morning, grabbed his sack lunch, and headed down the hall. On his way he joined two other juniors, Keyur and Rodney, and they talked about the Mets game. Nicolo left them as he reached room 104. It was a classroom that he and several other students use for tutoring during lunch hours.

Nicolo is tutoring William in freshman math. Every lunch hour, for 45 minutes, Nicolo and William eat together and study math. They have been doing it for two months now.

"Did you see the game last night?" Nicolo asked as he unwrapped his sandwich.

"I can't believe they pulled it out at the last minute like that!" William laughed as he chomped into an apple. He pulled out his homework and opened his book to get ready. They began working on fractional equations.

William flunked math last semester as a freshman. But at George Westinghouse Vocational and Technical High School, you don't really flunk. In the last few years, the school has been carrying out a commitment to having all children graduate and to providing them with the skills and knowledge they need for a successful life. So William was assigned to a volunteer tutor, Nicolo.

When they first began meeting for lunch sessions, William was skeptical. He had always been on the edge of passing or flunking. But it never seemed to matter before. They would just give him a grade and pass him on. What more did they expect of him? Did they think he wasn't trying? What made them think he was able to do any better than he always had?

Nicolo didn't give him time to ponder. He began each session by asking, "What are you doing in math today? What concerns do you have?" William would show him the assignments and would try to explain where he was confused. Nicolo would listen and ask questions that helped William talk through the problems himself.

When they finished the assigned problems, Nicolo would make up some more on his own, so William would get more practice. Sometimes, in

early sessions, William would say he understood it well enough and want to stop studying. But Nicolo knew he needed more work and talked him into continuing.

Nicolo encouraged William to talk with his teacher regularly to understand what was being studied, why it was important, and how it could be applied. Gradually, William became more and more comfortable with Nicolo and the tutoring process. He learned to communicate his questions more clearly, and best of all, he was making progress.

At the same time, Nicolo wanted to improve his tutoring abilities. So he began attending school meetings led by teachers and professors from the college across town. There he learned methods for effective instruction. The teachers asked the tutors how the students were doing and tried to suggest alternative learning methods.

At George Westinghouse, everyone understands that different methods work well for different kids. And everyone is looking for the best methods to reach those kids who are struggling. Everyone wants each kid to succeed. It is the goal of the school. Nicolo shares that goal.

William seems to sense that. He shows up every noon hour to meet Nicolo. And he always does his homework.

After about six weeks, William was nearly keeping up with the class. Nicolo decided to help him try a new strategy so he could do even better.

Why should William wait until he is behind the class and feeling left out? Why not work ahead of the class? That way when the teacher introduces something new, William will be hearing it for the second time and have a better chance of understanding it. Then he can interact with his classmates, sharing and learning with them, instead of always catching up.

So now, Nicolo has William ask his teacher what is next on the class agenda. And then they work on that material. Last week they studied supplementary and complementary angles. This week William is doing well with angles, right along with the class. It gives him a better feeling about the class and himself.

Both William and Nicolo are learning and improving themselves. Both are helping each other prepare for successful lives. And the whole school system is set up to enable and support them in that effort. A real lesson in *complementary angles*.

Discussion Starters

Concepts: aiming at a clear mission and vision; continuously improving everything we do; sharing power, ownership, and trust; encouraging teamwork; and making systems and processes work better.

Nicolo and William understood and shared in the school's vision that all kids should succeed. What do you think helped them see and share that vision?

What systems did the school have in place that supported and enabled the tutoring to happen and to be effective? Notice how much was happening with little or no adult guidance. What made this possible?

Compare a good-enough attitude to the persistence and continuous improvement that Nicolo pushed for. How did it make a difference for William?

More Ideas

In the Introduction, we said that our goal with *Kidgets* was to entice and excite. Hopefully, we have done just that. If so, we encourage you to learn more about the possibilities that this new approach to teaching, learning, and administration has to offer you and your school.

General Reading on Quality Improvement

Scholtes, Peter R. 1988. *The Team Handbook: How to Use Teams to Improve Quality*. The basics of quality improvement are described in this text. Also, the book details the mechanics of putting together a project team and building an improvement plan. The emphasis is on teams, with chapters entitled "Learning to Work Together" and "Team Building Activities." Available through ASQC Quality Press, 611 E. Wisconsin Ave., Milwaukee, WI 53202. Phone: 800-248-1946.

Senge, Peter M. 1990. *The Fifth Discipline: The Art & Practice of the Learning Organization*. While not addressing the specifics of TQM, Senge's book provides the philosophical underpinnings for much of the quality movement. His description of systems thinking—a way to view organizations from a holistic perspective—is particularly valuable to educators. Published by Doubleday and available at most bookstores.

Walton, Mary. 1986. *The Deming Management Method.* This book is written by a journalist and provides a general introduction to W. Edwards Deming, the man and his ideas. Deming's fourteen points are described in some detail. A number of case studies from service as well as product industries are included. Published by Perigree Books and available through ASQC Quality Press, 611 E. Wisconsin Ave., Milwaukee, WI 53202. Phone: 800-248-1946.

Books on Quality in Education

Bostingl, John J. 1993. *Schools of Quality.* The author introduces educators to the principles of total quality management and Deming's fourteen points. He advocates that schools move toward establishing processes that foster continuous improvement. Available through the Association for Supervision and Curriculum Development (ASCD), 1250 N. Pitt St., Alexandria, VA 22314. Phone: 703-549-9110.

Byrnes, Margaret, Robert Cornesky, and Lawrence Byrnes. 1992. *Implementing Total Quality Management in the Classroom.* This text clarifies TQM processes and procedures and demonstrates how they can be integrated into the classroom. Available through ASQC Quality Press, 611 E. Wisconsin Ave., Milwaukee, WI 53202. Phone: 800-248-1946.

The Educators' Companion to The Memory Jogger Plus+. 1993. *The Memory Jogger Plus+* focuses on seven quality tools to display verbal data. The *Companion* illustrates the purpose and use of the tools in a school context. Available through GOAL/QPC, 13 Branch St., Methuen, MA 01844-1953. Phone: 508-685-6151.

Fields, Joseph C. 1993. *Total Quality for Schools: A Suggestion for American Education*. Fields shows how the same principles that improve quality services and products in any enterprise also can be applied to American schools. Available through ASQC Quality Press, 611 E. Wisconsin Ave., Milwaukee, WI 53202. Phone: 800-248-1946.

————. In press. *Total Quality for Schools: A Guide for Implementation*. This book shows educators how to adapt the principles of total quality to school systems through a sequenced step-by-step method. Will be available in 1994 through ASQC Quality Press, 611 E. Wisconsin Ave., Milwaukee, WI 53202. Phone: 800-248-1946.

The Memory Jogger for Education. 1992. This is a special edition of *The Memory Jogger*, the pocket-sized guide to the seven basic quality control tools. It is designed to illustrate the tools—the flowchart, Pareto chart, cause-and-effect diagram, run chart, histogram, scatter diagram, and control chart—as they apply to school processes. Available through GOAL/QPC, 13 Branch St., Methuen, MA 01844-1953. Phone: 508-685-6151.

Neuroth, Joann, Peter Plastrik, and John Cleveland. 1992. *The Total Quality Management Handbook.* The handbook introduces the core total quality concepts of systems thinking, management by data, and continuous improvement. It also provides the Malcolm Baldrige Quality Award in self-assessment form for schools. Available through American Association of School Administrators, 1801 N. Moore Street, Arlington, VA 22209. Phone: 703-875-0748.

Rinehart, Gray. 1993. *Quality Education.* The author takes a comprehensive approach to education, offering ideas on how to improve the education system based upon quality principles. Appendixes address the special interest areas of values education and gifted and talented students. Available through ASQC Quality Press, 611 E. Wisconsin Ave., Milwaukee, WI 53202. Phone: 800-248-1946.

Schenkat, Randy. 1993. *Quality Connections: Transforming Schools Through Total Quality Management.* A special emphasis of this book is the use of the Malcolm Baldrige National Quality Award's criteria as a template for transforming schools. For example, sections discuss quality assurance procedures, human resource development, and information systems. Available through ASCD, 1250 North Pitt St., Alexandria, VA 22314. Phone: 703-549-9110.

Schmoker, Michael J., and Richard B. Wilson. 1993. *Total Quality Education: Profiles of Schools that Demonstrate the Power of Deming's Management Principles.* The authors offer an analysis of Deming's management principles and profile five schools or districts that have adapted these principles in diverse ways for carrying out their own improvement plans. Available through Phi Delta Kappan, P.O. Box 789, Bloomington, IN 47402-0789. Phone: 800-766-1156.

Articles

In the last several years some of the leading journals in quality and education have devoted sections of monthly issues to the topic of TQM. Here is a selection.

Educational Leadership, November 1992, has a large section containing eighteen articles entitled "Improving School Quality." Six are listed below:

Abernathy, Patricia E., and Richard W. Serfass. *One District's Quality Improvement Story.* This is a case study from a New Jersey school district. It focuses on one quality improvement effort:

to decrease high school tardiness and increase attendance.

Andrade, Joanne, and Helen Ryley. *A Quality Approach to Writing Assessment.* The TQM technique of measurement and analysis is used to improve an elementary school's writing program.

Bonstingl, John Jay. *The Quality Revolution in Education.* An overview of TQM principles with a series of TQM-in-action examples from schools around the country.

Harris, Melanie Fox, and R. Carl Harris. *Glasser Comes to a Rural School.* A Utah elementary school merges the ideas of William Glasser, site-based management, and control theory.

Hixson, Judson, and Kay Lovelace. *Total Quality Management's Challenge to Urban Schools.* The authors of this article describe how TQM principles can help city schools face unique challenges.

Another issue of *Educational Leadership*, from March 1992, contains a special feature, "Total Quality Schools," with three articles and an overview by the journal's editor.

Blankstein, Alan M. *Lessons from Enlightened Corporations*. According to the author, the formula for improving our schools can be found in Deming's fourteen points.

Bonstingl, John Jay. *The Total Quality Classroom*. The industrial model, with its top-down, authoritarian structure, has been dominant in education. A new paradigm is needed, and TQM principles provide a strong foundation for change.

Brandt, Ron. *The Quality Movement's Challenge to Education*. The editor of *Educational Leadership* concludes that American schools face the same challenges as American corporations.

Rhodes, Lewis A. *On the Road to Quality*. The argument is made that the reason TQM ideas are so powerful is because they are based upon popular culture. Much of it simply makes good sense.

Phi Delta Kappan, January 1993, has a pair of articles that address the quality movement in education.

Holt, Maurice. *The Educational Consequences of W. Edwards Deming*. The author's key point is that national reform based upon goals and standards is meaningless without reinventing the processes to achieve them.

Schmoker, Mike, and Richard B. Wilson. *Transforming Schools Through Total Quality Education*. After visiting a Toyota plant in Lexington, Kentucky, the authors suggest that educators study Deming because his work codifies what our schools need most.

Journal for Quality and Participation, January-February 1993, contains a section, "Visions of Excellence in Education," with eleven articles. Three are annotated below.

Ingwerson, Donald. *Participation . . . Beyond the Catchword Phrase*. The superintendent of Jefferson County Public Schools in Louisville, Kentucky, discusses how teamwork and participatory management have transformed relationships and work.

Rivers, Diane. *Creating Quality Middle Schools*. The quality initiative of the Birmingham Middle Schools—nineteen schools serving over ten thousand students—is described. The initiative is driven by Deming's fourteen points translated for education.

Tribus, Myron. *Quality Management in Education*. The author articulates three key quality principles for education. He also describes a series of problems and solutions in applying quality management in education.

The School Administrator, November 1991, has a series of five feature articles devoted to quality management in education.

Bender, Robert H. *If You Can Count It, You Can Improve It.* The superintendent of Crawford Central School District in Meadville, Pennsylvania, details his initial exposure to training and the use of teams and data to improve processes.

Melvin, Charles A. *Translating Deming's 14 Points for Education*. Deming's points are enumerated and illustrations are supplied from a Wisconsin consortium of four school districts that have adopted a TQM approach to teaching and learning.

Nyland, Larry. *One District's Journey to Success with Outcome-Based Education*. This is a basic review of the principles of outcome-based education. It fits well with the principles of TQM, which are centered more on processes.

Rocheleau, Larrae. *Mt. Edgecumbe's Venture in Quality*. The superintendent of Mt. Edgecumbe High School describes the approach by which students, teachers, and administrators have come to experience "shared responsibility" and the "joy of learning."

Senge, Peter, and Colleen Lannon-Kim. *Recapturing the Spirit of Learning Through a Systems Approach*. Systems thinking, a fundamental aspect of quality management, is a discipline for seeing wholes, recognizing patterns and interrelationships, and learning how to structure them in more efficient ways.

Brown, Enid Hilton. 1993. *The Deming Study Group of Greater Detroit White Paper: Exploring Dr. Deming and Education*. With assistance of The Deming Study Group and Dr. W. Edwards Deming, Brown explores the application of Deming's theories to education. Contact Brown at 30666 Oakleaf, Franklin, MI 48025. Phone: 313-737-0914. Fax: 313-737-2109.

Audiotapes/Videotapes

American Association for School Administrators (AASA). This organization has produced two audiotapes on TQM in K–12: "Quest for

Quality—How Total Quality Management Can Help Transform Schools" and "The Way of Quality—Conversations on the Enjoyment of Work and Learning." Each tape includes interviews with education leaders, teachers, administrators, and students who are involved in pioneering quality efforts in education. Available through AASA, 1801 N. Moore St., Arlington, VA 22209. Phone: 703-528-0700.

American Society for Quality Control (ASQC). ASQC has produced a videotape entitled "Continuous Quality Improvement: A New Look for Education." The video details how four school districts and one vocational-technical school have implemented total quality management (TQM) programs. Available through ASQC Quality Press, 611 E. Wisconsin Ave., Milwaukee, WI 53202. Phone: 800-248-1946.

"TQM in Education Videotape Series." A comprehensive package of fourteen videotapes that illustrate basic TQM concepts, the TQM process, its benefits, education's customers, individual roles, and so on. The series includes interviews with twenty-five school districts that are using TQM to improve their schools. Available through GOAL/QPC, 13 Branch St., Methuen, MA 01844-1953. Phone: 508-685-6370.

Networks and Newsletters

Koalaty Kid. This ASQC-sponsored network focuses on student-centered quality practices. It includes local business sponsors and advocates a broad-based partnership that reaches out not only to business but also to students and parents. For information contact Koalaty Kid, ASQC, 611 E. Wisconsin Ave., Milwaukee, WI 53202. Phone: 800-248-1946.

Quality Network News. This six-page, bi-monthly newsletter has such features as "From the Trenches," a column written by educators who are implementing TQM in schools, and "Talking Quality," a column contributed by quality management expert. For information contact AASA, Member-Customer Information Center, 1801 N. Moore St., Arlington, VA 22209. Phone: 703-875-0748.

TQM Education. The Association for Supervision and Curriculum Development sponsors a network on the topic of TQM in education. For information, contact John Jay Bonstingl, P.O. Box 810, Columbia, MD 21044. Phone: 410-997-7555.

About the Authors

Maury Cotter is an internal consultant with the Office of Quality Improvement at the University of Wisconsin-Madison. She has been instrumental in initiating and implementing quality improvement efforts at the university and at the state Department of Agriculture, Trade, and Consumer Protection. She has over 20 years of experience as a change agent in public sector organizations. She speaks and consults nationally for private and public sector organizations. Maury is a graduate of the University of Wisconsin-Madison with a degree in English. She is coauthor, with Lee Cheaney, of *Real People Real Work: Parables on Leadership in the 90s.*

Daniel Seymour is president of QSystems, a quality management consulting firm located in Palm Springs, California, and is a visiting scholar at Claremont Graduate School. He received his MBA and Ph.D. from the University of Oregon. Dan has worked in industry, and as a professor and administrator at the College of William and Mary, the University of Rhode Island, and UCLA. In addition to articles in leading education journals, he is author of the best-selling book, *On Q: Causing Quality in Higher Education* (1992), published by the American Council on Education and Oryx Press, and is coauthor of the 1992 Peterson's Guides book, *America's Best Classrooms: How Award-Winning Teachers Are Shaping Our Children's Future.*

LB2806 .C679 1993

Cotter, Maury.

Kidgets : and other
 insightful stories